Power Purpose Direction
Astrology for the 2020's

Power Purpose Direction
Astrology for the 2020's

By Jenni Stone

For permission requests, email **JenniStoneTheOne@gmail.com**

ISBN: 978-0-578-57297-0

Cover Image ID 270901 © Ice/Dreamstime.com

Printed in the United States of America

I dedicate
this book to
Henry

Acknowledgements

My sincere thanks to Paul Guttman - you talked me through the chapters. Your ideas added wisdom and insight.

Karrie, who made me a better writer, Brook and Paul who helped me to write Chapter 15: "Be You on Purpose," and Stephen who read Chapter 3 when no-one else could.

Thanks also to the many friends who offered encouragement - and to the superhuman editor and book designer: Cathleen O'Connor, who guided me through the publishing process.

Thank you.

TABLE OF CONTENTS

PART TWO

Introduction

This book is in two parts

Part One is a sequence of short chapters explaining astrology concepts in easy-to-understand language.

Part Two talks about the North Node in your chart.

That's where the magic happens. It's where you find your gifts, opportunities and challenges - and you don't need an astrology chart — you can just skip to the Appendix, look up your birth year and read the chapter for your Life Purpose.

It may take time to integrate, but when you see the power of being on purpose, you'll want to read the chapters for your children, loved ones, friends and the people you mentor, so that you can support and guide them with grace and wisdom.

This book can help you do your part.

This is me - doing mine.

Sending you Power, Purpose, Direction

Jenni Stone

Chapter 1 – The Coming Revolution

The coming revolution. Will it be blood in the streets?

The answer is yes, and in some parts of the world, there will be more, because tensions have escalated, the fabric of democracy is being stretched and we are asking:

Do we want to be guided by the best and most compassionate side of humanity – or allow our planet to be driven by toxic and uncaring leaders, tyrants and profit takers?

Many protests are about climate change - but other issues are coming up and while the rumblings have been there for years, the murmur of discontent has now become a thunder of concern. So … what is the source of this urgent worldwide call to action?

The next chapter talks about how the movement of the outer planets can trigger historical turning points, but first let's ask why the planets are so intent on bringing down governments and big corporations?

A Personal Story

In 2008 I was taking my seat on a plane and the man next to me showed me a magazine where he'd just had an article printed.

"I'm a conspiracy theorist," he told me.

"Interesting," I said.

"Yes. Like for instance I believe that it was the Bushes and the Clintons that got together to strategize this whole economic downturn."

"Interesting."

"Yes. They manipulated the financial markets and caused this whole housing and mortgage blowout to make themselves wealthy."

"Really?" I said. "And how did they get Greece to default on their debts…? And the stock markets to fall so catastrophically in England, Tokyo, and across Europe... and all within a few months? It wasn't a few families that got together." I said. His mouth fell open a bit. "It was bigger. Much, much bigger..."

His eyes got wide. "Shall I tell you who is responsible?" I said.

He nodded. "Yes."

"It was Pluto. Lord of the Dark Side; Harbinger of death and transformation and he said: "Enough of this over expansion, trees don't grow to the sky."

That was 2008 and it was Pluto who showed up to expose the corruption and fraudulent behavior of banks, mortgage companies and other Wall Street financial institutions. Integrity was tested — and it's about to happen again, but this time it's not just financial.

This time it's bigger, and we have a stronger line-up of planets saying that it's time for humanity to be troubled by children who are caught in a web of social injustice, the hungry, poor, sick, and those who don't have access to education — as well as being concerned for the environment.

Yes. It's uncomfortable to have the corruption and inhumanity brought to the light, but hopefully, after the revolution of the 2020's, we'll be able to build on stable and more sustainable ground.

We know, of course, that the rich and powerful are not about to let go without a struggle, but when Saturn, Pluto, the Sun and a cluster of other cosmic forces come together, there's no other choice and, starting in January 2020 the planets will move against what's unconstitutional, unfair, unethical and just downright insulting to our intelligence.

So...what's likely to happen in the 2020's?

My guess is that many multi-national corporations and authority figures that are not authentic will experience a shake-up.... and all this with Jupiter going into Capricorn (starting in December 2019) wanting a reset on the economy, which could bring down many oppressive regimes and perhaps, create a worldwide slowdown of the economy.

Do All Astrology Predictions Come True?

Sort of — but not always in the way you expect.

I have an astrology book from the 1970's suggesting that when Pluto went into Sagittarius (1990's) we would all want to launch ourselves into space.

Obviously, that didn't happen. We're still plodding along on Planet Earth, and yet, every morning, I use my phone to launch myself into Cyber Space.

Weird, yes... these predictions have a way of coming "true" in a way we could never imagine.

Hindsight is 20–20.

Why is Pluto getting involved and why is he so powerful?

Pluto is tiny and far away. Scientists will tell you that it's not big enough to be called a planet, but in astrology, Pluto wields great influence and the power comes from the fact that Pluto and its moon Charon are revolving around each other in a binary system.

They're almost the same size, with planet and moon always showing the same face ... and while our Moon is millions of miles away, there's not much distance between the surface of Pluto and Charon, so Charon appears to be a huge disc that's always hanging in the sky.

Perhaps that explains why this whirling dervish has such an impact on us, because after all, who isn't captivated (and energized) by something so bizarre.

Imagine watching the sky and seeing a large bird fly by. You might stop and look, but if two birds were chasing each other around in circles, you would stare at the spectacle... and this cosmic event is even more powerful because the Universe is energy, and this unusual "chase" stirs things up.

And... as Pluto hurtles through space, he sends out a message that you should transform your sweet self – and do it before he does it for you – because when Pluto gets involved, something has to die in order for it to be 'reborn' into a new and better version of itself. We're not talking about 'die' as in final death, but about transformation: of a relationship, a situation, or the existing version of yourself that has to perish so that the phoenix can rise from the ashes.

That alone would be enough, but the 2020 revolution is not just Pluto – it's also the line-up of Saturn, Mercury, Jupiter, the Sun and Ceres (the biggest asteroid) ... and it's not a one-time deal because from now through 2027 Saturn and Pluto will continue the work of changing the culture to create a more equitable society that's good for the majority – not just the privileged few.

A Footnote about Ceres

This was the first asteroid to be found and remains the largest. It was discovered in 1801 by Giuseppe Piazzi, a Catholic priest turned astronomer, who suggested naming the mini planet "Ceres" for the Roman earth Goddess and ruler of grain, the harvest, fertility and earthly renewal.

According to legend, Ceres was the mother of Persephone, the nymph abducted by Pluto to live with him in the underworld. Like any good mother, Ceres went searching for her beloved baby, and while she was travelling, the crops failed, and famine spread. This food crisis made Jupiter anxious and he was fearful that if too many people died, there would be no-one left to worship him. Egotistic maybe, but everyone wanted the King of the Heavens to be happy, and they needed Earth to be bountiful again.

So, with environmental issues in both heaven and earth, Mercury was dispatched to talk Pluto (his half-brother) and they struck a deal that Persephone would return to earth (and her mother) for eight months of the year and reside with Pluto during the winter.

As above — so below — and how appropriate that Ceres (the asteroid) should be in the mix when the cluster of Sun and planets meet up in January 2020. This proves, once again, that Mother Earth is truly a force to be reckoned with.

Chapter 2 – How the Outer Planets Change History

"If you want to find the secrets of the universe,
think in terms of energy, frequency and vibration."
-- Nikola Tesla

So... if everything is energy, we don't need to "see" the planets in our solar system, any more than a fish living in a pond would need to see a pebble that's thrown into the water. Just like the fish, we "feel" the energy sensations and know by the vibrations what kind of rock has caused the tremors of quivering power and, while we don't always recognize these signals on a conscious level, scholars and wise men have collected data for many thousands of years and have structured their findings into a logical system that explains how each planet generates a particular outcome here on earth.

These records evolved into astrology, which is slightly different across the different continents of earth, but each system has an underlying truth that every planet has a story to tell and a unique and distinctive signature of power.

The ancients didn't have telescopes to know that Jupiter is the biggest planet, but they recognized its expansive and extroverted nature.

They assigned Saturn, as the most distant planet that could be seen, (without a telescope) the role of setting limitations and boundaries, along with the authority figure that requires self-discipline.

Since then, we've added the nebulous frozen snowball that we call Neptune, the unique sideways spinning impulses of Uranus, and Pluto, which has the power to transform everything that it touches.

The bigger question is: by what means do we receive these messages?

Tesla said: *"My brain is only a receiver, in the Universe there is a core from which we obtain knowledge, strength and inspiration. I have not penetrated into the secrets of this core, but I know that it exists."*

5

Like Tesla, I believe that answers come from a Universal consciousness that's older and wiser than any individual human experience. We can argue whether this core influence is deliberately pushing humankind towards a higher evolution, or if it's simply an energy force that exists with no awareness or intention. In the end that doesn't matter.

Let's first acknowledge that it functions and that the messages translate into a collective urge to take action.

Collective versus Personal Predictions

Astrology says that there is free will on a personal level but when the energy of evolution dictates the outcome, it cannot be avoided. We know this because even the people who know nothing about astrology acknowledge that Mercury retrograde makes it difficult to close a business deal and, less well known, but well documented is the fact that Saturn often causes flooding on the first full moon after the winter solstice, or when it slows down to go either retro or direct.

Add to that, the ancient records that show Julius Caesar knew that it was foolish to begin a war when Mars is moving in retro because the outcome would be a humiliating defeat; but how about the distinctive watershed moments that change human history? Can those be traced back to cosmic "events?"

The answer is "yes"… and perhaps, it's these turning points that offer the best and most convincing evidence that astrology is authentic.

Looking back, we can see that the invention of the printing press, the industrial revolution and the spread of the Internet were each watershed moments that created a profound change in the way people behave… but what do they have in common?

Astrology notes that at the beginning of each revolution there was the conjunction (apparent meeting) of Neptune and Uranus in the sky and that pushed humankind into new patterns of acting and thinking.

In 1993 - 95 the alignment of Neptune and Uranus was the cosmic catalyst for the information and technology age.

The previous meet-up in 1821 (171-year cycle), was a major player in the industrial revolution and for the first time, machines replaced muscle power.

That innovation led to expanded trade, steamships that crossed the ocean, trains that spanned continents, and jobs in manufacturing that brought more population to cities and rural areas.

The 1650 cycle brought democracy and parliamentary process to England, and in 1479, this same cosmic conjunction fast-tracked the spread of literacy when the printing press turned out more than a million books across Europe.

What about other planets?

In the 1960's a completely different kind of energy flowed through the conjunction of Pluto-Uranus; a strong wind of change that brought sex, money, and rock-n-roll.

This radical thinking forever changed our culture by giving power to teenagers: enabling them to call the shots and dissolve the centuries-old paradigm of moral attitudes and male supremacy.

We are moving towards yet another significant turning point in the 2020s as the Sun, Saturn and Pluto come together at the sensitive degree of 22-3-4 Capricorn - with Jupiter, Mercury, and Ceres (the biggest asteroid), in close proximity.

As the combined power of inner and outer planets come together, it creates a pressure cooker of force and frustration that's calling for change in the way we treat women, minorities, and the dis-advantaged... and not just other humans, but also how we care for our planet, because it's all part of the same energy signature.

To voice our collective concerns, we're seeing brave and ethical leaders coming forward and using podcasts, cable television and social media to call for government that reflects the will of the people.

Will the 2020 revolution be blood in the streets?

Five years ago, when I first thought about the "revolution" of 2020, I was afraid that it would lead to violence and bloodshed, and indeed it has in many parts of the world as protests erupt in Hong Kong, Russia, South America, Europe and Puerto Rico.

What can we learn from history that can help us understand what's happening now? The last time this conjunction of Pluto-Saturn occurred at the sensitive point of 22-3-4 degrees Capricorn was in the 1600's when Martin Luther (the original) pinned his edict on the Church door and within months it went viral and swept across Europe, causing the protestant church to gain power. An even bigger impact was made when, for the first time, the Bible was published in a language other than Latin.

That was a big deal, because people wanted to read and be educated and that led to universities and higher education, teachers and writers making a living, and newspapers that created strong communities bound together by progressive ideas.

In the 1600's the only way to get the word out was to pin an edict to a church door, but now we have the Internet, TV, news outlets, social media and cellphone videos giving evidence of unrest. The mode of distribution is different, but the frustration is parallel to what happened in past revolutions.

What's likely to change in the next decade? We explored that in Chapter One, but for the moment, please know that the Universe will take care of this.

The 2020 line up of planets in Capricorn stands for eternal values and commitment to decent behavior.

It's taking a long time to get there, but history shows that tyrants come and go and regimes that are cruel and oppressive always fail...and right now, both the planets and the humans are saying "enough is enough" and corruption and inauthentic leadership is no longer acceptable.

The history-making line up of Sun, Mercury, Saturn, Pluto, Jupiter and asteroid Ceres together in Capricorn in 2020 would be enough, but there's also a Lunar Eclipse on January 10 (with Moon in Cancer) that adds a tsunami of emotional overload.

In the 2020's this is a cosmic message of frustration and protest that cannot be ignored.

Chapter 3 – The Astrology of Revolutions

"War is when the government tells you who the bad guy is.
Revolution is when you decide for yourself."

--Benjamin Franklin

Historically the scales have been tipped in the direction of male ego (conquest and winning) but our core values are shifting towards a more loving, compassionate place that values peace, education, healthy living, caring for children and the wellbeing of Earth.

The 2020's are a watershed

In chapter two we talked about how cosmic meet-ups between outer planets creates a spiral of energy that pushes humans into an evolutionary movement – and what's happening in the 2020's is somewhat similar to the Renaissance and the 1600's, when regular people (not just royalty and conquering forces) had a voice in where society was headed.

In January 2020 the line-up of Sun, planets and asteroids would be enough to do that, but there are two additional dynamics adding fuel to this rip-snorting energy.

One is the cosmic force of Uranus.

He ain't misbehavin' – this is just his way of clearing the decks for what's next.

As the modern ruler of Aquarius, Uranus operates as "The Awakener" that brings innovation, original thinking and an unshackling from the past.

This energy is a part of every revolutionary movement, from the French and American revolutions to the radical impulse of the 60's that changed music, architecture, sexual, and cultural norms.

Uranus is now moving through Taurus and in previous transits through this sign we saw:

- 1850 –59 – the rise of Communism – Napoleon's downfall
- 1932 – 42 – economic chaos following the 1929 stock market crash
- Second World War
- Japan attacked America in Pearl Harbor
- 2018 – 19 – sudden disruptions in financial markets, weather patterns and products of the earth like oil, gas and agriculture.

Not only that, but Pluto is at a critical degree – see diagram.

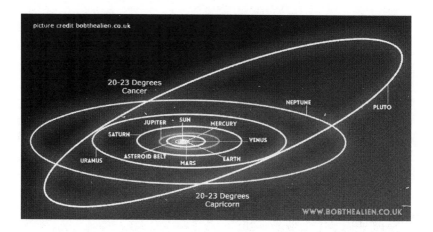

The energy of Pluto is always difficult, but when he intersects with the plane of other planets (20-23 degrees of Cancer and Capricorn) he becomes more unsettling.

Capricorn at 20-23 degrees was important for activating both the American Industrial revolutions and at the other end of the cycle, (20 – 23 Cancer) Pluto was also making trouble.

1932 – 1934

- Hitler became Chancellor of Germany and announced his war plans
- Gestapo secret police established
- Gandhi arrested and while in prison he went on a hunger strike
- Dust storms in Texas, New Mexico and Kansas turned the land into desert
- The great depression caused 33% unemployment in both Germany and the United States
- First Nazi concentration camp
- The famine-genocide in Ukraine reached its peak, with 30,000 deaths every day from man-made starvation.
- The Zeppelin air disaster

But this is also a story of how heroic leadership can turn adversity into redemption:

- Disgruntled farmers in Canada formed a political party, and despite having no organized structure, they won a third of the seats
- Franklin Roosevelt became US President with a plan to restore the economy.
- He said: *"We have nothing to fear but fear itself."*

2019 events – we've seen:

- Wildfires in California and the Amazon rain forest – icebergs melting – a summer heat wave across Europe.
- Man-made disasters – like pollution, toxic weed killers and plastic in the oceans
- Trade wars that put farmers out of business
- Tax cuts than only benefit big corporations and the wealthy
- People going bankrupt because they can't afford their medication
- Immigrant families torn apart by ICE police
- Immigrant children forced to live in cages.

Pluto is not the sole source of this disruption, but given what's happening across the whole world, it's an indication that the Universe is adding pressure for an evolutionary change.

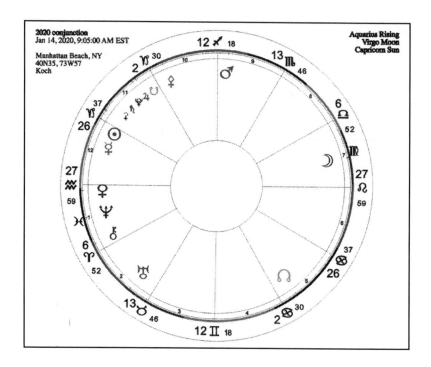

Predictions for the 2020's

When Pluto and other planets move into Aquarius, we are likely to see:

- A further blurring of gender lines and a more enlightened view of male-female roles - or being on the LGBTQ spectrum.
- Wearing technology to expand our five senses.
- A more flexible definition of work that's replacing the traditional one of having a job or career for a lifetime.
- Workplaces that are free from sexual harassment and corrupt leadership.
- Gender neutrality with men embracing their nurturing side and women free to pursue their dreams
- People taking responsibility for their emotional and physical health problems
- Grass roots organizations demanding that government authorities do their part to fix the issues
- A shift from power sources like oil, gas and coal to renewable energy

- Being spiritual rather than belonging to a religion - and making choices based on an internal moral and ethical judgment, rather than looking for guidance from dogma and outside (religious) authority.
- With this change in core values we'll see movies and TV entertainment making the transition from violence and guns to stories that are more intellectual, mindful, and curious.
- Freedom of the press and transparency about conflicts of interest
- World government? Not yet, but we're becoming aware (and passing judgment), on what happens in other nations.
- Self-care from holistic, natural cures, sound and energy therapy
- The return to moral behavior, self-restraint and taking responsibility for your actions
- Self-help books and on-line courses that bring self-understanding through astrology and ancient wisdom

Hot spots to look for in the cosmic cycles of the 2020's

December 26, 2019 - total eclipse of the Sun and meet-up with Jupiter that's close to the point of integrity (Winter solstice - zero degrees Capricorn).

The solstice is always a powerful position because it's where Earth takes a turn and begins the journey back towards the summer light (in the Northern Hemisphere).

Jupiter knows how to connect and hand out favors – but in the present climate – it's more likely to be punishment for people who've crossed over to the dark side.

The solstice stands for truth, wisdom, honor, self-restraint and setting boundaries – with a side order of callous uncaring for what has to fall in order for ethical behavior and traditional values to be maintained.

January 8 –15, 2020 – there are four planets and the Sun vibrating together to send out a once-in-a (human) lifetime slingshot of energy. Saturn, Pluto, Sun, Mercury and Ceres together at 23 degrees Capricorn, with Jupiter close by.

January 10, 2020 – Lunar Eclipse that adds angst and emotional drama to the monumental line up of Planets.

April 2020 - Jupiter and Pluto get together for another shout-out – which will most likely bring another round of protests and rallies.

June 21, 2020 — a total eclipse of the Sun as a bookend to the December 2019 eclipse; this time it's at the summer solstice point of 0° Cancer.

August to December 2020: Mars is entering and retrograding through warlike Aries bringing more delays and frustration.

December 2020: the Jupiter–Saturn meet-up at 0° Aquarius — ushering in the next (20 year) chapter of working towards more equality and social justice.

Uranus continues to do a crazy dance that brings wild swings to the financial markets and generates extremes of weather while he whispers: "it's time for a revolution."

Look for activity when Uranus stations in 2020: January 9 — 11, August 13 – 17.

2021 – January 12 – 20, August 18 – 22

2022 – January 15 – 18, August 22 - 26

2024 – Jupiter meets up with Uranus in Taurus. This is a replay of the cosmic events in 1789 that stirred up hungry French peasants, who were already tired of their out-of-touch monarchy — and that promoted the storming of the Bastille.

2027 - Pluto moves into Aquarius and amplifies the message of humanitarian and volunteer groups who advocate for equality, renewable energy, disadvantaged people and peace on earth

Chapter 4 – The Language of the Universe

"You have to know when to hold 'em – know when to fold 'em – know when to walk away – and know when to run."

--Kenny Rogers, *The Gambler*

Astrology: the deeper you dive, the more profound it gets.

It's the language that creation was written in, the blueprint that governs time, with:

- elements of physics
- quantum mechanics,
- mathematics,
- ethical behavior, and
- understanding of the higher vibrations of spirituality.

Astrology talks about how the cosmos works and the deeper you dive, the more profound it gets.

Where to start...it's easy to pick up on the moods and energies of the Moon as it passes through the signs and then to notice the change when the Sun and planets move into a different department.

You might also want to learn about your natal chart - which is the date stamp of energy that you were born into.

That chart, using the birth energies, along with some other proven techniques can tell you:

- your purpose and higher calling
- if you have gifts and superpowers that you're not using
- when and if you're likely to change location
- find a new group of friends that will stay with you for life
- experience a downturn in your finances

- if you'll change the direction of your work in the next few years.

Self-understanding and having a road map for the future makes you feel more self-assured.

It's the gift that keeps giving, but astrology can't tell you anything that's not true and that's because you look at everything through a filter of "is this me?" and you will reject what doesn't feel right — but there's a caveat, because understanding the natal chart is just the beginning of the story.

It's what you do with the energy that really counts and whether you claim the gifts, use the superpowers and make the most of the opportunities.

We talk about that in Chapter 8 because understanding the timing of the cosmos invites us to communicate, explore and collaborate in an intentional way.

Understanding how and when the planets move can tell you when to put your foot on the gas and when to pull back so that you can be in contact with the fabric of who you are when the busy whirl has slowed down.

You were, after all, born to be a human being, not a human doing.

Chapter 5 – Astrology and Symbols

"Other people may call that place the Avenue,
but I shall always call it the White Way of Delight."
*--*Anne, in *Anne of Green Gables*

Naming things has power. It's what allows us to distinguish between different ideas and concepts.

Naming a business is a key part of the branding process. Naming emotions helps us to the own the sensation and putting a label on behaviour such as male or female leads to a much larger landscape of ideas, personality traits, and ways of taking action – but words are not always enough and that's why astrology uses symbols.

The Sun, for instance, was worshiped as a deity for most of human history. It's the center of our Universe and without it's light, heat, and gravitational pull, we'd be a lump of dead rock wandering through space ... but how to describe the Sun in astrology?

The answer is that we don't.

We talk about the Sun through the seasons, like Sun in Aries or in Scorpio. In this way, the sign provides a context for the strength and power, rather like saying: President Ford or President Lincoln, because it's how the authority is used that defines the office.

The Moon is reflective of the position that she's in ("she" because being receptive is considered a female principle) and if the Sun is our calendar, then the Moon is the cosmic grandfather clock that ticks off time by moving from New to Full.

Fast-moving **Mercury** is the messenger in charge of travel and communications.

Mars represents the masculine effort we put into work, fighting, and competition.

Venus is feminine, receptive, and social.

Jupiter loves to travel and is expansive and optimistic.

Saturn embodies boundaries and limitations.

Uranus is freedom seeking, disorderly and disruptive.

Neptune transports us to a world of mystery, imagination and illusion.

Pluto and **Charon** working together are like a Trojan horse that invades quietly to bring down the established order and replace it with something more evolved.

Chapter 6 – What to Say to People who don't Believe

What to say when people give you that look that says: "*You don't actually believe in Astrology, do you?*"

I tell them that Astrology doesn't require faith, allegiance, or unthinking devotion. Astrology is not a religion. I would say that we know God had a plan because we're not living in some random collection of odd ideas that came together with no cohesive structure – and if astrology can help us to understand that plan, then it's all good. It is a roadmap to make your life better, like having an economic projection or the weather forecast.

Are the predictions 100% accurate? No. Only about 85-90% correct, but how many times can you afford to fail? As Benjamin Franklin said: *"An ounce of prevention is worth a pound of cure,"* and let's give him credit for choosing the date for the inauguration of the United States.

In the preface to his 1751 almanac, he wrote:

"Courteous Reader, Astrology is one of the most ancient Sciences, held in high Esteem of old, by the Wise and Great. Formerly, no Prince would make War or Peace, nor any General fight a Battle, in short, no important Affair was taken without first consulting an Astrologer, who examined the Aspects and Configurations of the heavenly bodies."

Then, perhaps I would talk about some other well-known people who've used astrology timing, like Walt Disney, who profited from knowing the right time to launch his movies and theme parks.

Ronald Reagan consulted his astrologer for the right time to sign film contracts and later she also advised Ron and Nancy on everything from the timing of his political campaign to negotiating peace deals with Russia.

Julius Caesar never went into battle without his astrologer; and Cleopatra, who had the zodiac symbols carved into her palace, sent her favourite astrologer with Mark Antony when he returned to Rome (mostly to spy on him).

In the fourteenth century, Queen Elizabeth the First delayed her coronation for a year on the advice of her astrologer, because she wanted to help her loyal subjects through the difficult schism between the Protestant and the Catholic Church after her father (Henry the Eighth) broke away from traditional religious practices.

Good Queen Bess restored order, made her country wealthy, and became the strongest military force in Europe; and she was tremendously popular, despite her refusal to get married and produce children.

She said: *"I know I have the body of a weak and feeble woman, but I have the heart and stomach of a king, and of a king of England too."*

And, if they're still listening, I would tell the story about Alexander the Great, whose birth was timed by his father because he wanted a strong warrior and hero and, to achieve that, the royal astrologer suggested waiting until Mars would be in Taurus for the birth. With that schedule in mind, the King timed the conception (hopefully with the agreement of his wife) and, when she was ready to give birth, a servant was sent out to watch for the moment when Venus would be visible in the night sky. Everyone in the palace was waiting, and when the sky watcher yelled: "Tell her to push. Tell her to push now," the midwife encouraged Alexander's mother to get with the program.

History confirms that the King got his wish and Alexander came out bold, brave, and good looking (Venus rising); and yes, he exceeded all expectations and built an empire that stretched across two continents, earning him the title "The Great" because he never lost a battle, despite being outnumbered most of the time.

And let's not forget that J.P. Morgan famously said that astrology is not for millionaires, it's for billionaires.

If that's not enough, I might talk about the 5,000 years of data that's been collected by some of the greatest minds that ever lived, including Plato, Socrates, and Sir Isaac Newton.

You don't have to believe in astrology for it to work.

It's practical strategy that connects everyday events to the symmetry of universal timing. It's cosmic harmony in what often feels like a chaotic world, along with some really good guidance for the road of life. Wouldn't you want to know the best time to send out marketing materials, sign a contract, start a project, or make friends? Or if your finances are about to take a downward spiral and it's time to do something sensible to protect your assets?

It is your choice whether you put your confidence in astrology or not.

Chapter 7 – Cookbook Astrology

What is "Cookbook" Astrology?

This is a way to learn astrology by taking note of the "ingredients" in a chart. It is rather like learning to cook by studying recipe books and watching videos to acquire the skills.

Astrology is more challenging than food preparation and there are more variables. Everyone has to start by learning the basics: the symbols and traits for twelve signs (Aries through Pisces) and, from there, the properties and energy signatures for the Sun, Moon, and planets. After studying this basic information, we start to take in aspects, houses, elements, ruler-ships, chart patterns, mutual reception, and the psychological aspects of character that come through various alignments. This basic information is available through books, websites, on-line courses, and from listening to blogs and talking to other astrologers.

But astrology is so much more than ingredients! It takes into account the whole chart and the dynamics between the Sun, Moon, and planets. So, let's imagine that you have flour, eggs, and raisins and could bake something up. It might end up being a pancake, a muffin, or an elaborate birthday cake, and you just don't know until you've put together the rest of the ingredients.

So, let's look at an actual chart and learn what we can from the ingredients:

Joe Biden was born November 20, 1942 at 8.30 am in Scranton, Pennsylvania. His Sun is closely conjunct Venus and a bit separated, but still in Scorpio, with Mars; which is all much concerned with work and service to others. This is a theme that is also echoed by the Taurus Moon in his sixth house.

Joe has a mostly above the horizon chart with 15% fire, 15% earth, 20% air, and 40% water elements – suggesting that he relates through feelings, heart, and emotions. His North Node is Virgo, which you can read about in Chapter Six. The strong Mars in Scorpio would suggest dynamic action, motivated by progressive and passionate personal power.

His Ceres (see Chapter 1) is in the fourth house of family, ancestor roots, and shared experiences, and when you put that together with the strong urge to be of service, you can understand what makes Joe run. It is not from ego or a need to be famous, but rather from a deep commitment to do the right thing for his family and community. However, if you were looking at this chart without knowing who it is, you wouldn't know if this person was serving his country on the front lines - a pioneer in energy healing – or perhaps someone who stayed in their home town and worked to help people who are homeless and disadvantaged.

Astrology has answers for both personal and collective understanding, so please use this wisdom to get clear on your unique power, purpose, and direction. From there, use it as a parent, to support and encourage; as a leader and mentor, to help those who look to you as a guide; and please add your voice and actions to help make the decade of the 2020s a turning point in history towards a better and more humane society.

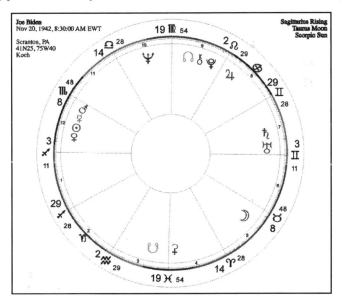

Chapter 8 – Cosmic Timing

"You are the navigator, the captain, and the ship."
--Vera Nazarian

The one thing successful people have in common is that they know where they're going, and they radiate confidence — and confidence is the lifeblood of success. It makes you bold and willing to try new things, ready to look for creative answers and offer encouragement to others.

Nothing succeeds like success, and as Tony Robbins says:

"People who succeed have momentum. The more they succeed, the more they find a way to succeed. Similarly, when someone is failing, the tendency is to get on a downward spiral that can become a self-fulfilling prophecy."

This is especially true if you're doing the right thing at the wrong time because you may start thinking that you're not good enough... and while failure is said to be good for you, too much and you start to feel defeated.

It's much easier to stay the course if you know that you'll be successful in the future. (Yes, astrology can tell you when.)

Astrologer Evangeline Adams helped JP Morgan and Charles Schwab to amass vast fortunes. She predicted the stock market crash of 1929 and told JP Morgan not to go on the maiden voyage of the Titanic because she cast charts for the ship and the journey and felt that it wasn't safe.

Corporations, Royalty, heads of state, Julius Caesar, The European Union and the Catholic Church all used cosmic timing to start projects and find the best time to appear in public...and we don't hear about it because the astrologers are sworn to secrecy

President Reagan kept quiet until a member of his Cabinet and Time magazine revealed their secret and later his daughter, Patti Reagan David wrote in her book. *The Way I See It:*

"My parents have done what the stars suggested—altered schedules, changed travel plans, stayed home, cancelled appearances."

Want to know when the good days are coming, so that you can plug into that positive energy?

Yes, you do… because the difficult aspects show up as the times when a car skids into your driveway, knocks down your mailbox and collapses into a pile of scrap metal.

The positive, constructive days are not so obvious and unless you know when to grab hold and use this energy to structure a social event, business plan or marketing strategy, those times can float past in a bubble of agreeable feelings.

Timing is everything… Well maybe not everything, but when you know what's ahead, you feel more confident.

" We ask ourselves, who am I to be brilliant, gorgeous, talented, fabulous? Actually, who are you not to be? Your playing small does not serve the world."

--Marianne Williamson

Chapter 9 – Mercury Retrograde

Mercury Retrograde is a bad time to buy a car or a cell phone

"If you can't explain it to a six-year-old, you don't understand it yourself."
--Albert Einstein

Let's first ask the question: How can Mercury stop, stand still, and go backwards? If a plane or a bird did that, it would fall out of the sky.

The answer is that it only appears to be that way from Earth and if you've ever sat on a train that's pulling out of the station or in a car going forward when the traffic lights change, you've seen a similar illusion.

Of course, the Greeks and Romans didn't have trains, or cars, or planes, but they knew that Mercury is pretty perverse when he's going in the wrong direction. It's not a good time to travel or put forward ideas for regulation, because during that time, deals get stuck and tend to go around in circles.

So…OK…That's the first thing to know.

Mercury only looks that way from Earth, but the effects are real and can be very annoying. But why is this a bad time to buy a car or a cell phone? I would have thought it had more to do with when these things were manufactured than when the contract is signed.

In Chapter 2, we talk about how we're living in a Universe where the movement of planets generates waves of energy that communicate and connect.

Seen in that light, the planets are not hard-surfaced balls of rock rolling around in space, but clusters of wave-like energy, each carrying a unique signature. That means we're living in a Universe that shares information and catches conversations between the Sun, Moon, and other planets.

Why Mercury Retrograde is a bad time to sign a contract.

Contracts are "real." Agreements have consequences and when created in good faith, they create a blip of energy that lives on, and this is especially true if you've agreed to buy a product or service that provides transport or communications, which are both in the domain of Mercury.

Everything is related, but some things are more specific than others.

The next question is why some retrogrades are worse than others? And the answer is that Mercury is making a transit to your natal chart.

What's a transit?

That is when the planets "out there" are vibrating at the same frequency as your internal rhythm and that message of energy acts as a distinctive wake-up call.

That "something" could be a shout-out from a friend, loved one, or someone you've dealt with in business who is now reaching out to say: "I was thinking about you." It could also be an agreement, a legal issue, or a project that's taken a long time to come to fruition and is finally ready for closure.

How does Mercury know which "strings" to pull?

He doesn't, and it's nothing personal.

Try to imagine that we're all floating around in an ocean of energy vibrations, and there are "hot spots" that have additional power because an important event or meeting occurred at that position. It's rather like a radar screen where there's a bright blip of power that's left over from something in the past and that "blip" lives on and carries the signature of that event.

So… OK… now Mercury comes along and finds that exact location to re-activate an event that happened in the past.

That's a transit, and the energy is even more vigorous when he stops to turn either retrograde or direct (makes a station), because, from our point-of-view on earth, the little winged messenger is slowing down and almost at a standstill and the resonating energy makes a deep and lasting impression which, if it's located close to a sensitive place in your natal chart, will create a situation that's life-changing and could take you in a whole new direction.

Yes, it's important to know if you're likely to be caught up in one of these cosmic events but to understand when (and what), is likely to happen, you need help from an astrologer that's been practicing for a while and knows how these things play out.

So ... what about when Mercury is moving at a normal speed in retrograde?

That acts like a time loop, and it's (sort of) the equivalent of cosmic therapy.

It's a way of bringing back the past so that you can look at the places where you've been hurt either by others, or through your own behavior.

Revisiting the Past

As humans we'd rather keep going forward and don't willingly go back and look at events and people that have caused damage but when they come up during a retrograde, we may have to re-examine these episodes so that what's broken can be restored. And we do it because that's how, with compassion and forgiveness, we rebuild ourselves and restore others on the journey.

And this is especially important in this modern, fast-paced world, because to achieve any good level of success it's necessary to come from a place of wholeness, rather than a place of being broken and wounded.

So... don't kill the messenger, which is another way of saying don't blame the Mercury retrograde and instead, be open to seeing the past in a different way and be willing to reconcile, rebuild, and transform what has been negative into a more positive light for the future.

And I'm telling you this because the Universe is going to do what the Universe is going to do - and it's up to us to find the positive and make the best of it.

Oprah said: *"Turn the wounds into wisdom"*

Good Things to Do During a Mercury Retrograde

- Get in touch with people you haven't seen for a while
- Look for customers that didn't buy the first time
- Visit friends and family
- Edit, revise, and re-vision
- Avoid starting new endeavors, but this is a great time to finish up anything that's taken a long time to reach fruition.

- Real Estate: negotiations may get bogged down during the retrograde
- Retail: you may experience more returns than usual.
- Health: best if you can avoid surgery and other elective procedures, unless you're going back for a corrective fix.
- Do something different and meet new people. They may not be in your life permanently, but will often stay in touch and want to meet-up again when Mercury again retrogrades; and remember that things that are lost during the Mercury Retro are almost always found, so if you've misplaced an item don't worry, it will turn up.

More Good Things:

- Think outside the box, develop intuition and be creative
- Change habits and thought patterns; do some soul searching
- Resolve old conflicts.
- Tie up loose ends, finish projects, and complete any long overdue assignments.
- Don't start a new business – or do a major expansion for an existing one.
- Instead, renew, revise, rethink, reorganize, reflect and get rid of anything that no longer serves you.

Chapter 10 – Mercury the Myth

In Greek mythology he was the winged messenger that carried the office memos between heaven and earth. Pictures of him show a handsome, athletic guy wearing a brief toga to show off his six pack and well-muscled legs. He's in a hurry (as usual) to deliver messages and his winged feet are lifting him into the sky.

As an infant, Mercury was known for his lively wit and quick answers and he was often in trouble for playing pranks and stealing.

He took a sword from his half-brother Mars, a trident from the hand of Neptune, and the royal scepter from his father and when he got caught Mercury made everyone laugh so much that they forgot to punish him.

His father was Jupiter, King of all the gods and everyone knew that if he took you out to dinner, he'd always pick up the tab.

Jupiter fathered many children and one of them Minerva according to legend, was born out of a splitting headache. . . more likely Minerva gave him a splitting headache when she appeared, fully grown, and said: "You're my Daddy."

As for Mercury, according to folklore, his mother was one of seven heavenly sisters that Jupiter seduced and worse, one version says that he did it while they were asleep, which these days could get you into serious trouble but back then was passed off as "boys will be boys."

But either asleep or awake, Jupiter's wife Juno soon learned of the affair (after all, it's difficult to ignore a handsome bad-boy winged messenger who flies around heaven all day), and in a fit of jealous rage, she transformed the seven sisters into the star cluster of Pleiades

Despite the fate of his mother and apparent disregard of his father, Mercury was happy, though perhaps in need of therapy as he can sometimes be perverse and tricky (in retrograde).

He kept busy, carrying messages and, in his spare time, took on the job of looking after business, financial gains, theater, and thieves - and what do those things have in common, perhaps an element of illusion or trickery?

Mercury was also known for his storytelling and for being a talented musician and, despite his bad habits, much loved as a companion to heroes, friend to the lonely, and a helpful guide to travelers.

It was Mercury who proposed the idea of putting up signposts at crossroads and he also inspired the custom of giving thanks by placing a stone at the base of the post, which helped to clear the fields of stones, and provided the building materials to pave the highway.

Mercury the Planet

- About the size of Earth's Moon
- Solid rock, and cratered surface
- From the surface of Mercury, the Sun would appear to be three times bigger, and hotter, than from Earth and since it's constantly in the stream of solar winds, Mercury has very little atmosphere of its own.

Mercury doesn't rotate and because one side always faces the sun, and the other is always in darkness, there's a hot, brightly lit side and another side that's cold and dark.

This contrast in temperature supports the two-faced nature of Gemini (ruled by Mercury), and, if you are fortunate enough to have a Gemini friend, you'll know that they have a 'good' side to their personality and a badly-behaved side…. a sort of Jekyll and Hyde twin that gets them into trouble.

In Astrology, Two Signs Are Ruled by Mercury

Gemini, the quick-witted mercurial messenger with dozens of close friends.

Virgo is more practical, thoughtful and sensible. The myth of Mercury almost exactly describes Gemini, but Virgo is an earth sign with a mind that's more practical and methodical, and yet both signs are in serious trouble when the little winged messenger goes into reverse gear and does a retrograde.

So, there you have it, Mercury the myth and the signs he rules and what I find astounding is that both Roman and Greek mythology almost exactly describe the nature of Gemini (the sign) without a telescope to know the properties of Mercury, the planet.

Chapter 11 – Was there a YOU Before You Were Born?

Was there a "you" before you were born?

Have you ever looked into the eyes of a baby and said: "that's a blank slate waiting to be told what to do, feel, think and what kind of personality to have"… ?

Of course not.

Everyone comes to earth connected to their family and astrology says that you choose the time of your birth, your parents, and the circumstances that you grow up in.

Of course, as a child you don't get a lot of options. If your parents divorced, you suffered. If your family moved to a different neighborhood, you had no choice but to go along, but that's not the end of the story because you have free-will and as you grow up, you can decide whether to use challenges in a positive way or say: "I got dealt a bad hand and I'm going to complain a lot but not do anything about it."

All that pre-supposes that there's an inner "you-ness" that's already developed and shaped; an identity that's formed and won't accept outside opinions.

If you're smart, you will want to know more about that inner "you-ness" and what the Universe believes you are capable of (with the help of people who believe in your greatness) … along with an understanding of the challenges you've had to go through.

From there you can figure out what has impacted your personality from the outside. Let these beautiful words of Courtney A. Walsh help you remember:

Dear Human

Dear Human: You've got it all wrong.
You didn't come here to master unconditional love.
That is where you Came from and where you'll return.
You came here to learn personal love.
Universal love. Messy love. Sweaty love. Crazy love.
Broken love. Whole love. Infused with divinity.
Lived through the grace of stumbling.
Demonstrated through the beauty of... messing up. Often.
You didn't come here to be perfect. You already are.
You came here to be gorgeously human.
Flawed and fabulous. And then to rise again into remembering.
But unconditional love? Stop telling that story.
Love, in truth, doesn't need ANY other adjectives.
It doesn't require modifiers.
It doesn't require the condition of perfection.
It only asks that you show up. And do your best.
That you stay present and feel fully.
That you shine and fly and laugh and cry and hurt and heal
and fall and get back up and play and work and live and die as YOU.
It's enough. It's Plenty.

--Courtney A. Walsh

Chapter 12 – Unseen Energy Vibrations

"The best and most beautiful things in the world cannot be seen or even touched -- they must be felt with the heart."
--Helen Keller

The question is: are concepts like ethics, peace, struggle, failure, hope, triumph, and compassion built into the Universal consciousness?

I'm asking because these ideas don't have substance in the "real" world and they only exist within the invisible energy of the collective, but without these principles, life would be unbearable, and Earth would be a terrible place to live.

To find answers we have to look beyond science, religion and the traditional belief systems that we've come to rely on.

If we turn to Eastern philosophy like Buddhism, they would tell you that love is nirvana and you should meditate the problems away, which to me is like saying "Go stick your head in the sand and you too can be happy."

If we ask scientists to explain love, they might say that it's dopamine and neurotransmitters firing off to ensure reproduction of the species.

Karma – what's that? Is there a judge and jury in some eternal place that decides what thoughts, events and actions deserve retribution and if so, when will it catch up with the real estate client that cheated me out of several sales commissions?

There's also the Western (manmade) concept of an eternal God who created the universe out of nothing, which is difficult to swallow because given the immense willpower that it took to create the Universe out of nothing, you'd think that this God-like presence would be more efficient at promoting peace and good will on earth.

In past times we might have been willing to accept these authoritarian ideas, but in the 2020's we're questioning more deeply. So, let's begin by looking at some of the ways that we perceive these unseen energy vibrations:

Telepathy happens faster than the speed of light, like when you're thinking about someone and the phone rings

Music is not just sound. Music can bring you to tears, lift you up with joy and evoke strong memories.

Devotion is a tangible force that has you willing to walk through hell for the ones you love.

Loyalty and commitment are the glue that holds the world together.

Compassion can change not only your life, but also the lives of the people that you touch.

Mindfulness alters your immediate perception of everyday living.

The light of understanding instantly transforms what was murky into something brilliant.

Our natural world restores and realigns the anarchy of overthinking into a more harmonious and graceful alignment.

Intentions can overcome fear because when you decide to work at something that you're passionate about, you create an unseen, but powerful force that turns into a heat-seeking missile on a mission.

The arts can take us on a journey using the vehicle of a painting, a song, dance, or the story of a courageous hero that makes us hold our breath in anticipation. The book is real, the performers are real, but the narrative is the bridge that moves ideas from the world of creative energy into what we think of as "real," and that begs the question: "What is a story, and why do the good ones have such power over us?"

Prayers can move energy when you're sending positive thoughts to help someone through a difficult passage.

What's happening when you meet an old soul and sense that you're on the same page or **thinking that you've known someone for a lifetime** though you've only just met?

When you are talking to a old friend like no time has passed, though it may have been years since you connected?

There's the logic of knowing that when someone dies their whole personality and the lifetime of effort doesn't just disappear like a puff of smoke. We know there's a lingering energy structure that remains intact even when the body is no longer alive because spirit visitations are only possible if there's an afterlife.

How about **walking into a room** and getting a good or bad "vibe" and feeling the residual mood in a space where people have been angry?

The body chills when you know something to be true, but there's no way rational way of knowing.

The body language that doesn't start in the body ... it starts in the mind with attitude, but what's attitude? Where does that come from? Is "attitude" your lifetime habits showing up as confidence or lack of it? More likely it's a mixture of your personal history, your mindset and your view of the world from the inside out, with perhaps a smidge of residual energy that's left over from your time between lifetimes.

Life Purpose is another concept that doesn't exist any place that we can reach by the five senses but when you get it, there is a deep, inner ringing of bells that continues to resonate long after you've digested the information on an intellectual level.

I believe that all this invisible energy is how we're connected to the Universal Consciousness and maybe...just maybe, it's these dynamic forces that stop the universe from flying apart.

These are all good questions and I hope that in writing about this, I have opened a portal that makes you less afraid to share your own experiences.

There you have it. We've examined the afterlife, telepathy, body language, love, and the vibe in the room and ... by comparison, the idea that planets in space are sending out waves of energy and messages... seems almost mundane and obvious compared to the effect of these unseen forces.

As John Lennon said: "*The more real you get the more unreal the world gets.*"

Part Two

The Revolution is Coming, and YOU have a Part to Play

Chapter 14 – Doing Your Part

"Politicians are like diapers and need to be changed frequently."
                                        --Attributed to Mark Twain

What will you say when your grandchildren ask?

"What did you do in the revolution?"

"Did you march and protest?"

"Did you speak out against poverty, inequality, injustice and bad behavior?"

"Were you on the right side of history?"

That last question is the most crucial because the next seven to ten years are a pivotal time for all humans on this planet and while it's not comfortable to live through, changes need to be made – the earth's climate has to be stabilized and a more just and equitable future established for everyone.

It's no accident that you are alive at this time and while we can't change the position of the planets, we can choose to support the coming revolution by sending the message that humankind is headed in the wrong direction.

This is bigger than one election or which political party you vote for.

Throughout history we've seen that power corrupts and that's why. Given a choice between democracy and autocracy, people will choose to have free and fair elections, to remove those who are duplicitous in the way they use their power, money and authority.

The danger is that inertia and apathy will sideline the process – or that money and political contributions can influence the outcome.

What you can do

- When necessary, cast your vote outside your usual party lines
- Question the ethical and moral standards of leaders that you are voting for
- Do your best to resist advertising, cult brainwashing and propaganda.
- Send positive energy, thoughts and intentions to support the fearless leaders and organizations that are fighting for reform.
- Talk to people you know but also be open to those who challenge you.
- Use your creativity: writing, artwork and illustrations as a way to reach others.
- Learn to present your ideas in writing and in person in a compelling and visionary way.

"If not us, who? If not now, when?"

JFK and others said it, but this question is significant now that we have the heavyweight cosmic forces lined up to help humanity see that ageless values are not based on money – but rather on consciously and deliberately seeking out wisdom, decency and respect for all human life - and that it's necessary to love humanity, even when individuals are misguided.

Chapter 15 – Be YOU on Purpose

"Everyone has a calling and your real job is to figure out
as soon as possible what that is and who you were meant to be."

--Oprah

What is your life purpose and higher calling?

The ancient Greeks called it "daimon." In Egypt it was the "ka" with whom you could converse. Plato used "Paradeigma," a force that is the bearer of your fate and fortune. Perhaps the modern spiritual equivalent is your "higher self," a guide and companion on the soul's journey towards enlightenment that helps you to find ways to serve humanity.

What's for sure is that you need to be somewhat awake and mindful to know that such an influence exists because for many people, the guidance seems to lie dormant while for others, it's so strong that it doesn't allow much departure from the path.

Unfortunately, life doesn't come with an instruction manual and sometimes it's only by seeing the reaction of others that you can judge if you're doing it right.

It's like you're wearing a tee-shirt that says: "I'm here to do x, y, and z and if I do it right, give me a hand-shake and congratulate me but if I'm doing it wrong, let's both feel uncomfortable."

The problem is that there's no way to articulate what "it" is… ah, but there's a way to know for sure because when you're doing it right, that inner purpose becomes your source of power and people quickly recognize that in you and come forward to give you encouragement, support, energy and opportunities.

This book is your guide and, while it may not tell you everything you need to know, it can tell you if you're going in the wrong direction.

Start where you are.

Use what you've got and find how you can contribute.

Look for your birthday and read your chapter - you don't need to consult an astrologer or read a chart.

Awareness is the first step – intention follows – and when you're going in the right direction, we need you to add your voice, purpose, and energy to the revolution of the 2020's.

Play your part in the coming revolution

Your impact and involvement come in three parts: be – do – and think about the kind of leadership that will get us there.

What are the qualities we want to see in our leaders?

We need decision-makers that bring good judgment - grounded on intelligent assessment of the situation rather than ego, or alignment with political, racial or religious beliefs.

Leaders who speak truth and can make us feel connected in a heart-centered way, but who are still humble enough to say: "I know that life is valuable because I've seen suffering, and I know what happens when people are broken."

We want integrity, accountability and a desire to make a difference – because that's what makes heroes out of regular folk and champions out of crusaders.

If you are that leader, please come forward to motivate others. You don't need to run for high office, just be your authentic self and make a difference.

What you can do:

In your garden and environment:

- If you need to use fertilizer – use organic
- Avoid weed killers and especially Roundup as it's toxic and causes cancer.
- Compost and recycle food scraps
- Bee keeping
- Stop watering your lawn, grow food or let it go wild.

Food choices

- Buy local and organic food that's farmed without synthetic (human-made) pesticides, herbicides and fertilizers.
- Cut down on sugar

- Go more towards vegetarian – the meat in just one beef hamburger can pollute 1800 gallons of water.
- Avoid buying from farming practices that keep animals in cages. It's cruel to them and unhealthy for you.
- Avoid preservatives and additives like: Sodium Nitrite - Monosodium Glutamate (MSG) - artificial food coloring - High Fructose corn syrup - Aspartame. - BHA & BHT.
- Shop in stores that care and, whenever possible, buy glass containers rather than plastic.

Recycle clothing by donating and then shopping for used items

Reduce plastic bags and tableware by putting reusable bags in your car and asking your take-out places to stop the plastic.

Donate to your local food pantry and volunteer your time and energy to help out.

Use renewable energy – at present, only 11% of power comes from renewable sources.

- Consider making your next vehicle electric or hybrid. Vehicles are now available from Nissan, Mitsubishi, Renault and Tesla -and other automakers are planning to make models available soon: Jaguar, BMW, Honda, and Chevrolet

Be more of you:

- For the holidays – make the decorations and give something you've created or crafted.
- Walk as many places as you can.
- Be present, be mindful and make a conscious decision to sometimes disconnect from news media and tech devices.

Be a voice for future-think

Speak to your legislatures, school boards, and city councils. Trickledown economics doesn't work and neither does top-down policy decisions about the environmental issues.

Talk to your local church (which pays zero property taxes) and ask them to open their doors to the community for health clinics, tutoring centers, safe spaces and gardens.

Be You on Purpose

Align your destiny with the coming revolution.

This is important because we're at a moment in history when we need to question authority, recognize what's inauthentic and defeat the liars, narcissists and showoffs - by revealing them for what they truly are.

ACTION STEPS for the times we live in:

"I believe the problems of human destiny are not beyond the reach of human beings." John F. Kennedy

JFK had to be pushed to run for office, but as President he supported public housing, civil rights and immigration.

His Life Purpose (Chapter 26) was to be a combination of down-to-earth sensible and future oriented visionary - to reach across obstructions and break through glass ceilings - not just for himself, but to also make space for others to follow.

Find your Life Purpose – learn about your own power, purpose and direction – and then do it for friends and loved ones so that you can parent and mentor. Offer advice without being critical, help to lift them up when they're struggling, show compassion when they're stuck and give wisdom and support when they're looking for a change of direction.

Chapter 16 – FAQ about the North Node

Is the North Node the same as my sun sign?

No. This part of your life blueprint shows up on your chart as a symbol and looks a like a horseshoe with a circle at each end.

What does the North Node look like? Is it a planet?

It's not something that exists as an actual physical body. It's a mathematically calculated point where the Moon crosses the "line" of where the Earth-Sun plane would be.

If you imagine that the Earth and Sun are at same level, like a flat dinner plate, then the Moon would sometimes be above and sometimes below that flat (but invisible) dinner plate.

It's only when the Sun, Moon, Earth line up exactly that there's a total eclipse, but as we know, that's a rare event. However, if you calculate where the Solar Eclipse would occur on a flat surface, that's where the North Node sign would occur. (Yes, it's complicated.)

The North Node indicates your Life Purpose.

Is my Life Purpose the same as my vocation or job?

It's more about your inner calling. For instance, you could be a doctor that helps out in a third-world country – or a doctor that goes on TV to sell a treatment for acne. Both have the credentials of being a doctor, but they each work to serve a different purpose – and depending on your Life Purpose, it might actually be right for you to be the doctor that makes millions by going on TV.

Can I find my Life Purpose by filling out a questionnaire like Meyers-Briggs or Strength Finder?

No - in fact you'll get exactly the wrong answers that way. Those tests are designed to get information about who you are now, not who you need to become in order to reach your greatest potential.

When I understand my Life Purpose, what will happen?

As you become more aware, you will reach for different goals and there will be shifts in your routines and habits.

What can I expect once I'm on the right path for my life purpose?

Loved ones will open their hearts and celebrate the progress, because when you're being authentic and stepping into your power, relationships get better.

There may also be some criticism, and that's because some people will see your growth as a problem.

Will there be other changes?

When you're moving in the right direction and your behavior supports your life purpose, the doors open, and people come forward to support and encourage you.

Start where you are, use what you have and enjoy the journey.

How about my work?

There will be a shift in the way you work, maybe not your everyday job, but you'll get greater understanding of what makes you passionate, what feels meaningful and how you can make a difference.

What's amazing is the speed that things can happen, because when you understand your life purpose, the energy around you changes, you get wings and the power to go in the right direction.

What if I have the same North Node life purpose as someone I know?

That person will resonate with you and most likely you'll have passion for the same pursuits, have similar gifts and strengths, and you 'talk' the same language at a soul level.

The challenge is that while you can mirror each other on same issues, if one of you is NOT moving in the right direction, it will get difficult. You might try to tell them that they're doing it 'wrong' ... that they just don't get it ... and you might say all that while not being able to articulate exactly what "it" is.

This book can help because once they know their North Node, the path becomes clear and most likely they will say: "Oh yes, I knew that..."

What if they don't get it?

That leaves them stuck, and that could create some distance, not because they can't understand, but because you do.

How many different Life Paths are there?

Twelve, one for each sign, and the North Node stays in the same sign for about 18 months and then goes to the previous sign (it moves backwards) and returns to the original position every 18-19 years.

Why haven't I heard about this?

Many astrologers don't mention the North Node because it's difficult to explain.

What do other books say?

Some talk about soul purpose, karmic mission, lunar nodes, and the dragon's head. If they do mention the North Node, it's only a brief paragraph or two and, while all that other stuff adds up to self-understanding, we're living through times of historical change and need to play our part by living our power, purpose and direction.

Chapter 17 – ARIES North Node

*"Understand that your experience facing and overcoming
adversity is actually one of your biggest advantages."*
--Michelle Obama

YOUR LIFE PURPOSE – as seen through your Aries North Node:
YOUR GIFTS AND STRENGTHS

- You are charming and get-along well with others
- Discreet and can keep secrets
- When offering criticism, you're sensitive and diplomatic
- You are good at seeing both sides of the situation
- You speak truth while still being agreeable and good-natured

At work - you know how to negotiate. You collaborate, reconcile, and come up with solutions that are fair on both sides.

In relationships, you tend to fit in and play fair, listen to ideas, and appreciate how others operate.

The challenge is that in the past, you have asked permission, followed the rules, and been the peacemaker, and this behavior has shaped your relationships, and made you so sensitive to how others feel that alarms go off as soon as you see conflict.

By wanting approval and being willing to step back in order to maintain the peace, you've allowed others to define you, not by what is good for you but by how much you can contribute to their wellbeing and peace of mind.

All of this may have worked for you in the past, but now you need to find your own frequency and not be afraid to take up space knowing that the greatest gift you can offer is to teach the rest of us how to be less afraid of being strong, unique, and pioneering.

Your LIFE PURPOSE is to find your authentic, one-off identity and to be independent, self-aware and NOT have your happiness be dependent on others, but rather to look to your own desires, goals, and satisfaction.

In the past you've probably worked at making others happy by being tactful and diplomatic and perhaps you've buried yourself in books or writing, wanting to enjoy a quiet and comfy routine, thinking that as long as you don't make big waves that this quiet lifestyle could be maintained.

Later in life (or perhaps by reading this book), you've come to realize that people have their own problems and while in the past, you've had to be emotionally self-sufficient, now is the moment for you to stand up for yourself and be willing to hear some opposition and criticism.

That doesn't mean you should never compromise but please know that the very people that you need to stand up to are the ones who are expecting YOU to be self-sacrificing and give yourself over to their needs, and now you need do this because your power and purpose comes from discovering your own strength of will, to making a commitment to initiate action and demonstrate a more assertive side of your personality.

ACTION STEPS

Think of yourself as the hero, ready to set out on an adventure and live a bigger life.

- Start by noticing any patterns of suppressing and denying your emotions, especially anger and resentment
- Find work or a project that makes you feel alive and keeps you motivated while you let go of what's not working.
- Validate your needs and perhaps keep a journal (or put up sticky notes) to remind you of WHY you're taking action.
- Create a routine and prioritize the things that please you, even if that's difficult at first
- Notice where you're allowing yourself to be manipulated
- Plunge in, take action, and speak your mind, even if it gets an angry reaction

- Be decisive and don't second-guess yourself, even though it may lead to a not-so-good outcome because at least it will be YOUR outcome, not the result of vacillating and sitting on the fence.

If there's someone that is difficult to confront you could rehearse the scene and imagine having their face in front of you while you talk back. This might seem like nothing but doing this will change your internal vibration; and that can alter the dynamics of the relationship.

The paradox is that good people and loved ones are waiting for you to take control. They want you to take charge of your own life and they will endorse and celebrate your power, purpose, and direction because you stood up and took charge.

EARLY LIFE

You may have been in circumstances where you seemed to have little or no power.

You may have felt the need to make your parents happy, or perhaps you were protecting someone else by acting as a buffer to keep family life intact and it's also possible that you were at the receiving end of terrible abuse or perhaps you witnessed abuse in your family and were afraid for your own safety.

This bad treatment may have carried through into an early marriage, partnership, or situation where you remained hidden instead of expressing your own thoughts and opinions.

These early situations meant that you allowed others to make decisions and perhaps you kept quiet and sacrificed something of yourself to maintain harmony.

That was a brave choice at the time – but it's now important to make decisions that put your needs and desires in first place.

What you can do today that will change your life:

- Practice saying "No" to assignments that are not in your best interests.
- Notice who is trying to make you do something that benefits them and not you
- Look for situations where you can act independently.
- Give yourself permission to not accept any task or project that doesn't further your priorities

- Recognize your inner strengths and find situations to break out of the routine.
- Move on and let go of what happened in the past.

The future is waiting for you - and it will be different.

RELATIONSHIPS

Others see you as sometimes saying: "No problem, come closer" and other times saying: "Go away."

And when they're not sure what answer they'll get, it can be difficult to sustain a relationship.

The paradox is that others are waiting for you to take charge and set the rules.

You could say something like: *"Look, I want to spend time with you, but I need to complete this project, so let's get together tomorrow at 3pm and we'll go to the park and spend a few hours having fun."*

There. You did it. You just set the agenda. You gave a specific time and a start and finish.

You're in charge and while you may not be able to achieve this level of control every time (and may have to stand up to some people who are used to getting their own way) it's important for you to move in that direction and accomplish as much as you can.

You could start by taking control in some situations - watch to see how others react and, on an inner level, look at the stress factors — and especially any fear of being alone.

Romantic situations can be difficult for you

Even after you've resolved the inner issues, marriage and intimate relationships can still be difficult.

You may be afraid of being swallowed up or having someone run your life.

Many people with your Life Purpose find it difficult to give total commitment so they maintain a separate home or live together without the legal ties of marriage.

The commitment of a relationship requires balanced energy between two adults and that's never easy, but more difficult when you're afraid of commitment.

The good news is that you may not be the problem but you're 100% of the solution.

Just know that being afraid and being in a victim mode, tends to attract predators and that could become a lifetime problem that can only be resolved with outside help.

ACTION STEPS:

- Create a stable routine for yourself and a place to go where you can feel comfortable.
- Be aware of internal feelings that come up
- Look for situations where you can be strong-willed, original and independent
- Define your unique contribution
- See to your own needs and be more assertive in going after your objectives
- Express yourself in a more forceful manner
- Get up the nerve to go after the relationship that you most desire – and when you find it, be honest, direct and straightforward. Put a high value on commitment, expect support and encouragement and don't take betrayal lightly.
- Know that it's OK to be a bit eccentric and break the mold of what's expected
- Don't be fearful about having negative emotions
- Take your physical, mental, and emotional health seriously and try to work through negative reactions with an exercise routine that will turn mad into muscle.
- Get things moving in an enthusiastic, energetic, whole-hearted sort of way
- Overcome restrictions that you've put on yourself and the limitations that others have placed on you.
- Don't second-guess yourself. Be creative, curious and in-the-moment with each project.

In Business – this is the time for engagement, working towards a measurable outcome, and going from innovative idea to achievement. The power of your Life Purpose is to take action, pursue what matters, and become the innovative way-shower and leader that motivates others.

The challenge is that you might have to start the journey without a plan and have to learn new skills even if you are not quite ready but isn't that true for everyone when they first start out?

People who share your life purpose:

These are some of the well-known and celebrated people who share your **Aries North Node** Life Journey.

What they have in common is their purity, honesty, and innocence but we also see a quiet determination to be heard, a hero's voice that speaks out despite the prevailing narrative of their time.

Julia Roberts, Sean Connery, Richard Gere, and Cybill Shepherd.

Some had difficult childhood experiences, like Julia Roberts, who left home when she was a teenager because her relationship with her stepfather was so damaged.

Sean Connery was painfully shy, and Richard Gere avoids talking about his early years.

Cybill Shepherd says it all in her autobiography: "*Cybill Disobedience. How I survived Beauty Pageants, Elvis, Sex, Bruce Willis, Lies, Marriage, Motherhood, Hollywood, and the Irrepressible Urge to Say What I Think.*"

Julia Roberts in *Pretty Woman* won both critical acclaim and the hearts of American audiences as a streetwalker, introduced to high society by her co-star, Richard Gere. In the movie, Julia walks a tightrope of being sexually provocative while being charming and innocent.

In the movie, Julia's character, true to her Aries North Node life path, refuses to accept the position of doormat and mistress.

Winston Churchill was born two months premature at a time when most preemies didn't survive and although he was not physically strong and often severely depressed, he was rebellious and was often punished at school for being outspoken.

His mother rarely visited him at boarding school, despite his letters begging her to either come to the school or to allow him to come home. His relationship with his father was a distant one, and they barely spoke.

His closest relationship was to his nanny, whom he used to call "*Old Woom*".

Churchill ran for office at the age of 25, determined to warn people of the evils of the Nazi regime, which he saw as a relentless war machine that would one day try to invade England.

His speeches in Parliament were widely reported and he eventually persuaded the government to prepare for combat.

After an Allied victory he famously said:

"This is not the end. It is not even the beginning of the end. But it is, perhaps, the end of the beginning."

Fred Rogers – his TV program for pre-school children was simple and direct. It didn't feature animation or the fast pace of other children's shows.

Dorothy Parker – both husbands were alcoholics and the second was gay. She drank to excess and made four suicide attempts.

She died in 1967, leaving her entire estate to Martin Luther King Jr.

"If you want to know what God thinks of money just look at the people he gave it to."

"I like to have a martini, two at the very most. After three I'm under the table, after four I'm under my host."

"The cure for boredom is curiosity. There is no cure for curiosity."

Julia Child – chef, author and TV personality. Her book, *Mastering the Art of French Cooking* was reprinted 19 times and became a best seller again with the release of the movie, *Julie & Julia*.

At the beginning of WWII Julia was told that being 6 ft 2 made her too tall for the army, so she joined the civil service and was soon promoted to top-secret research.

That was where she met her husband and together, they moved to Paris where she learned to cook.

Lisa Marie Presley - her parents divorced when she was five and Elvis died when she was ten.

As the sole heir to father's millions, she has control of his estate and with her mom's guidance, has grown it to more than $100 million.

At twenty, she married for the first time already four months pregnant, but the couple later divorced and now her ex-husband lives in the guesthouse of her California home.

Three months after her divorce became final, Lisa married Michael Jackson, but the tabloids assumed it was a publicity stunt to improve his image after the accusations of child molestation. They dissolved their marriage amicably after a year.

Lisa Marie is now healthy, private and reclusive. She attends the Presley Enterprises board meetings with her mother.

Others who share your Life Purpose:

Meryl Streep, John Lennon, Queen Victoria, Rachel Ray, Will Smith, Sammy Sosa, Lucy Liu, Michelangelo, Neil Armstrong, Ray Charles, Sigmund Freud, Stevie Wonder, Sir Christopher Wren, Sir Richard Branson, Della Reese, Cybil Shepherd, James Earl Jones, Toni Morrison, Martha Graham, Larry Hagman, and Stewart Granger.

WHAT'S NEXT?

- Take time to think about this until you experience the inner 'knowing' that this is your purpose, destiny and direction.
- Talk about these goals. Be bold and assertive and don't be afraid of getting a negative reaction
- Find a circle of enthusiastic admirers who applaud your courage
- Acknowledge that you haven't always been the daring pioneer that you were meant to be, but that now you're moving in a good direction.

"One of the greatest gifts you can give anybody
is the gift of your honest self."

--Fred Rogers

Chapter 18 – TAURUS North Node

*"I have a dream that my children will one day live in a nation
where they will not be judged by the color of their skin
but by the content of their character."*
--Martin Luther King

"I tried being reasonable. I didn't like it."
"I have a very strict gun control policy;
if there's a gun around, I want to be in control of it."
--Clint Eastwood

YOUR LIFE PURPOSE – as seen through your Taurus North Node:
YOUR GIFTS AND STRENGTHS:

- Resilience and the ability to move on after difficult experiences
- Knowing that, with sensible planning, you can get through a crisis
- Understanding of universal truth and wisdom
- Seeing where you might have compromised in order to fit in or be taken care of
- Having the depth of character to notice when you're excessively suspicious about other people's motives or being too emotionally dramatic.

At work - you have a reserve of strength, you're organized, restrained and can work under pressure.

Your LIFE PURPOSE is to create a calm and joyful home base, be a peacemaker for others, and establish financial security for yourself.

And when you feel valued and appreciated: to have the courage to talk about the difficulties you've experienced, resolve any unfinished business and then move on without being angry or accusing.

To get there, you need to find that bedrock of self-worth, overcome the crisis situations of the early years, and find a reserve of strength to create a loving place of harmony in your home and life.

But it can't just be any life — when you're doing it right, others look to you for wisdom as a leader and way-shower and that means you have to be at the top of your game.

To make progress you may need to create order, let go of emotionally overloaded situations, avoid jealousy and deal with anything that stops you from living well and being a source of joy. You may need to learn to trust again, to have faith that your needs will be taken care of and develop skills for taking care of money and other resources, both for yourself and for others.

You might also want to take an interest in conservation and protecting earth's resources as these are also forms of "wealth" that need to be protected.

It's also important to embody the less visible signs of affluence:

- Being kind and forgiving
- The calmness of faith and assurance that things will work out
- Consciously knowing and setting a standard for beauty
- Artistic creativity
- Logical organization of resources
- Time management
- Your unique grace in being able to carry through with your good intentions because you're coming from a place of calm abundance.

And doing it by losing the drama and being peaceful, steadfast, and a source of joy, love, and support to those who need help — which is pretty much everyone because we're living in chaotic times.

EARLY LIFE

You had a deeply rooted need for love, approval, and gentle affection.

You believed that the world is a good place and that others would do right by you.

Perhaps you allowed them to set goals and formulate a strategy for you and maybe this meant you had to live through crisis situations, loss and separation, anxiety over money and uncertainty about the future.

More than all that, you may have felt hurt, disappointed, and betrayed because those you trusted didn't live up to your high ideals

Perhaps you still haven't fully separated yourself from those early problems and are more focused on the betrayal than on your own healing.

In extreme cases, this could have taken you into an early marriage or into relationships that were difficult, painful, and unsustainable.

Yet despite all these challenges, you're such a good person that you remain hopeful and are willing to forgive.

It's important to maintain that attitude of release, as long as you're doing it from a place of strength, safety and comfort where you're surrounded with people who are emotionally supportive and encouraging.

As Gandhi said: "*The weak can never forgive. Forgiveness is the attribute of the strong.*"

You may not be there yet, but when you can acknowledge the past but not let it define you, then you can see how far you've come in creating your own self-worth and can take ownership of the poise and dignity that is the hallmark of your Taurus life purpose.

ACTION STEPS:

- Recognize and honor your need for a calm environment.
- Create a place in your home where you feel comfortable, safe, and able to enjoy the abundance of both material things and financial stability.
- Practice saying: "I need to have a say in what goes on."
- Walk in nature.
- Slow down and enjoy the moment.
- Notice that when you compare yourself unfavorably with others you feel insecure - but when you validate your own strength, you're a winner.

Enjoy Life:

- Give full attention to your senses.
- Enjoy art, music, literature and natural beauty.
- Read a romance novel and imagine yourself the main character, swept along by passionate urges and fully engaged in intimate moments.

- Smile at strangers and hug friends
- Act like you're rich and in love
- Be generous and forgive, forget and bless those who've wronged you.
- Dress up in something flowing and luxurious.
- Cook a sumptuous meal, light candles, and play love songs
- Reveal your most intimate feelings to a loved one.

In Business:

Give yourself permission to refuse to take on any task or project that could create a crisis situation.

Notice what work makes you feel fulfilled, especially when you help others by offering opportunities in a way that's fair, ethical, accommodating and generous, knowing that those qualities will bring loyalty and assistance when it's needed.

It's important to work at your own pace, because you have more purpose, resolve, and determination than you ever thought possible.

Remember that when you feel hurt because others are critical or get too involved, you can go to your "Zen" place and ask them to "back off."

"Until a person can say deeply and honestly, "I am what I am today because of the choices I made yesterday," that person cannot say, "I choose otherwise.""

--Stephen Covey

RELATIONSHIPS

Are better when you can establish boundaries and are able to state clearly when the other person has gone too far. This helps to release any need to judge and instead, helps you to move on and put energy into your own needs.

Your Challenge is that your intense emotional desires can take over and make you crazy.

It's easy for you to see through others and penetrate their motives but you might be less aware of your own unconscious patterns and can't see what's holding you back.

Please notice that sometimes you get caught up in feelings of jealousy, envy and suspicion and the problem is that being overly possessive will make loved ones want to run away, rather than stay and live with your distrust.

Leave behind:
- Crisis Situations
- Over-reacting
- Having to destroy something in order to eliminate one part or piece of it
- Any obsessive worry, fears, or compulsive behavior
- Situations where you feel that you're being duped or becoming a victim.

Enjoy a feeling of fulfillment knowing you're having an influence on the lives of the people and realizing that you're not just giving, but also getting back.

It's important that you create structure so that you can take time off and not let work be your only reason for living.

You have many choices. You could be working in the financial advisory business, or have in a career that has to do with the beauty of nature, art or material objects or you could choose to put your efforts into environmental issues and let that become your life work.

For you, it's not just what you do. It's also that you make full use of your skills, creativity, management abilities and inner gifts and do it without allowing others to crowd you or make you feel less than powerful.

Remember that you're best in situations where you can be in charge of your immediate environment.

It is important for you to set (and maintain) boundaries whenever you feel any sense of danger or being uncomfortable.

You could either work for yourself or find a good fit where you can have some control and can maintain a calm environment.

Make it a practice to check in and ask yourself: "do I feel safe, comfortable, and protected?"

If you're in the business of things like cars, real estate, or appliances make sure that you have a solid base to work from with an office that's comfortable, has easy parking and good equipment.

If you are selling services - show that you have a history and a future. Assure clients that you will be there for the long term, that you will be effective, and provide first-class treatment, good judgment and have concern for their timetable and comfort.

Money

You've probably been in circumstances where your finances were in jeopardy but to honor your life purpose, you need to calm down, take care of yourself and know that, if similar circumstances ever came up again, that you wouldn't allow yourself to be hurt.

Feeling wealthy by enjoying the abundance.

Enjoying the senses: food, art, music, flowers, massage and luxury items such perfumes and lavish fabrics.

Celebrating the growth and the milestones.

Having a sense of gratitude for what you have and all that you've achieved.

People who share your life purpose:

Perhaps, like Tennessee Williams and Stephen King, the emotional crisis of early years has carried over, always there and threatening to pull the emotional rug out from under you.

Or maybe, like Audrey Hepburn, and Prince Harry, you've chosen to overcome the drama and stress of early experiences and have moved on to have a meaningful life.

Many had to overcome difficult early experiences that could have broken a lesser spirit while others got themselves into messy situations and then had to listen to public disapproval.

Grace Kelly, Audrey Hepburn, Clint Eastwood, Cindy Crawford, Jacqueline Kennedy Onassis, and Nicole Kidman. They all have dignity, poise, and they don't complain, don't explain, don't gossip or write kiss and tell books. Instead, they put the past behind them and create meaningful lives.

Eckhart Tolle — much of his early childhood was in post war Germany playing in bombed out buildings while his parents fought and eventually divorced.

He moved to London and started working as a teacher while he studied Hindu, Buddhist, Jewish, and Christian early texts but at age 29, became unbearably depressed and quit his job. For about two years he sat on park benches, living rough, staying with friends or at a Buddhist Monastery.

His family thought him "irresponsible, even insane." Later he wrote about the inner transformation that he went through, saying: *"If I complain enough – the Universe will do something about it – thus proving that unhappiness works and will brings change – but as an adult I have to see that that it only makes things worse."*

What he's trying to say, is that being attached to a problem keeps you chained down, so that you keep circling back rather than being free to pursue your own dreams and desires.

Tennessee Williams – at five, a childhood illness paralyzed his legs, and he was bedridden for nearly two years. His mother, who was smothering and probably suffered from a mood disorder, gave him a typewriter and encouraged him to make up stories.

His father, a traveling salesman, became increasingly abusive, especially towards his older brother. His sister was schizophrenic and institutionalized, and we can see the cruelty and inhumanity of this childhood reflected in his plays, like: "A Streetcar named Desire", and "Cat on a Hot Tin Roof."

He said: *"There is a time for departure, even when there is no place to go."*

Paulo Coelho – as a teenager, he told his mother that he wanted to become a writer, to which she responded, "My dear, your father is an engineer. Do you actually know what it means to be a writer?"

At 17, his parents committed him to a mental institution, from which he escaped three times before being released at the age of 20. He then went to law school to please his parents but dropped out after a year.

He later remarked that: *" They didn't do that to destroy me. They did it to save me."*

He sold the rights to his best-seller *The Alchemist* to Hollywood for $29M.

Clint Eastwood grew up introverted and self-reliant, qualities that are the repeating theme in his film roles where he stands for what's right.

Martin Luther King – minister, and leader of the Civil Rights movement.

His father regularly whipped him until he was fifteen, and a neighbor reported hearing the elder King tell his son that: "he would make something of him, even if he had to beat him to death."

At age 12, and in a deep depression following the death of his maternal grandmother, he jumped out of a second-story window, but survived.

Bouts of depression continued throughout his life and yet he found the courage to start a nonviolent, civil disobedience movement based on the principles of Gandhi. He said: *"I have a dream that my children will one day live in a nation where they will not be judged by the color of their skin but by the content of their character."*

Not everyone is so serious: P. J. O'Rourke – Journalist.

His masterwork was: *"How to Drive Fast on Drugs While Getting Your Wing-Wang Squeezed and Not Spill Your Drink."* This work appeared in the *National Lampoon in the '70's.*

Others Who Share Your Life Purpose:

Ronald Reagan, Barbara Walters, Oscar Wilde, Jeremy Irons, Harvey Milk, Lady Gaga, Ted Danson, LeBron James, Anne Frank, Benjamin Franklin, Thomas Jefferson, Prince Charles, and Mother Theresa.

WHAT'S NEXT?

- Take time to think about this until you experience the inner 'knowing' that this is your purpose and direction.
- Know that your self-worth is counted - not only in material things – but also by the example you set for others by being loving, and forgiving
- Surround yourself with people who support and encourage you
- Acknowledge where you've missed the mark but you're still trying
- See yourself as the spiritual architect and gardener that shapes souls
- Recognize that you've done a lot right and that you're moving in a good direction.

"Self-acknowledgment and appreciation are what give you the insights and self-awareness to move forward towards higher goals and accomplishments."
--Jack Canfield

Chapter 19 – GEMINI North Node

"See yourself as a work in progress."

--Brian Tracey

YOUR LIFE PURPOSE – as seen through your Gemini North Node:
YOUR GIFTS AND STRENGTHS:

You're exuberant, speak with authority and can tell the truth in way that isn't spiteful or hurtful to others, but rather in the spirit of sharing what is apparent to you, but may not be so obvious to them.

You pay it forward to help others and are good at creating admirers (and sometimes critics), but no matter the response, you remain engaged.

You have an internal ethical and moral compass that guides you, yet at times, this can also make you less tolerant of others who don't share the same values

- You are optimistic and have a philosophical outlook
- You attract friends from all over the world and travel easily.
- You have an awareness of technology, social sharing, and pop-culture, and you know how to capture the values, ideals, and the attitude of your generation.
- You expand your horizons through education, travel, exploring foreign cultures, and bold thinking.

At work – you are good at creating educational programs that help people to connect and investigate ideas beyond their immediate circle of friends.

You enjoy meeting new people through networking, marketing, and making deals.

Your idea of relaxing is seeing an action movie, hero adventure, or by exploring new cultures and cuisine.

Your LIFE PURPOSE is to communicate, be fully engaged, and bring your wisdom and good judgment into everyday situations.

At your best, you are tolerant, good-natured and allow others to have their shortcomings without judgment or feeling superior.

At your most annoying, you barrel through and use your considerable strength of will to enforce your ideas and assessment of the situation.

This is worse when you give a negative response to a loved one, or when you remain stuck in your beliefs and make others feel "less than."

It's important to stop thinking that you're the expert or guru, the sole authority that has all the answers instead of being diplomatic and presenting your ideas in ways that others can understand — and then staying with it until they engage and grasp the concept.

This is difficult as you very much want to be accepted but, to get there, you have to relate one-to-one, not as a teacher, authority figure, or with a sense of entitlement but instead, by finding common ground with regular people.

If you can do that, you have the potential to be an inspiring trailblazer and influencer for your generation, but that's not easy for you as leadership requires restraint, self-imposed boundaries and putting the needs of others ahead of your own.

To get there, tell yourself that it's OK to be vulnerable. You're allowed to have limitations and needs and it's acceptable to be highly functional and still be in need of support and encouragement.

Let your defenses down sometimes and be human because no-one who has ever lived has done it right every time.

It isn't weakness or failure. We're all in this together, fumbling along and co-operating on the road to find love and acceptance.

Your greatest potential is to connect and pull together your tribe with easy collaboration, so that you can function from a place of non-judgment, where everyone's happy, relaxed, and emotionally healthy.

Please know that this is one of the more difficult Life Purpose directions because it's never easy to go from: "I'm right... and you need to listen to me" to:- "Tell me what you think about this . . . ?"

EARLY LIFE

As a child you were excited about learning. You brought philosophical humor to any situation, and you engaged others with your charismatic personality and gift for easy dialog.

This made you seem persuasive and engaging, but sometimes that came through as aggressive because you acted as the authority, wanted the last word and were unwilling to back down.

In school and later, in college, friends were important as you learned to network, socialize, and find courses to develop your academic, business, and professional skills.

As you got older, you made adjustments, and began to appreciate that there is not a single set of rules that everyone is following.

Now perhaps you're slowing down and seeing that your bravado and proclivity for having daring adventures is not always so comfortable and that you might want to fit in and be part of the crowd.

Of course, to get this insight you don't have to fail miserably or play this out on a world stage with an audience.

Most likely there will be watershed moments when you realize that you don't have all the answers and this leads to a series of adjustments where you find that speaking your mind and having to be 'right' can obscure your other good qualities and cause people to back away.

One of your great strengths is your willingness to learn and you could see this as an opportunity to engage:

- Slow down, listen and be present
- Learn to accept other people's points of view
- Allow for an exchange of ideas, opinions and belief systems without judgment or thinking that you have all the answers
- Avoid roles where you need to provoke or be competitive
- Stay relevant and on-task.

ACTION STEPS:

- Practice saying: "I'm interested to hear what you have to tell me."

- Notice where you are dominating the conversation and find a way to ease your foot off the accelerator.
- Know that the best way to have influence is to listen to other people's points of view and let them open up and be understood.
- See that you can learn not just from those who are highly intelligent and educated, but by meeting everyday people at every level of society.

At work:

- You're creative, know how to communicate, can effectively use technology and social media and instinctively understand the attitude of public opinion and present-day culture.
- You know how to reach a mass market and this, along with your unique (and entertaining) point of view, makes you a sure-fire front-runner in today's world.
- You're at your best in situations that allow for an exchange of ideas and it's best for you to stay away from tasks that are repetitive and boring.
- You find freedom and adventure by taking short journeys and quick getaways.

Leaving behind:

The need to be right or pre-judging the situation.

Arguing about the argument instead of working towards a resolution.

Taking shortcuts and thinking that you already know the other person's plans (or viewpoint).

And most of all: having blind trust and uncritical devotion to a cause, guru, religion, corporation, or social movement.

Your greatest potential is to teach from the heart, in a loving way by meeting people, not as a teacher, coach or trainer but as an influencer that is willing to listen and be respectful of other points of view.

RELATIONSHIPS

When you were young you were restless, needed to travel and learn for yourself firsthand how the rest of the world lived.

This need for freedom may have inhibited early relationships and made you wary about intimacy and the traditional roles of marriage and the responsibility of having babies.

Fortunately, the success (or failure) of a relationship is judged only by two people and not by how society sees you.

That's a good thing, because in today's world, you are less restricted and if you decide that a traditional white picket fence is not for you, then you're free to choose a less conventional lifestyle.

PEOPLE WHO SHARE your Life Purpose:

Mark Zuckerberg, J.K. Rowling, Steven Spielberg, and Bill Clinton.

They all instinctively know and can articulate the mood of their audience.

Zuckerberg created Facebook while still in college, thinking that it was a great way to get to know other students and now it's the world's biggest media company and remarkable for NOT owning the content, but instead being an outlet for others to speak.

PEOPLE with your Gemini Life Purpose WHO ARE STUCK in the "I'm right - and my opinion is the only one" mode:

Kim Jong-Un

Mitt Romney

O.J. Simpson

Donald Trump.

Here are some of the well-known and celebrated people who share your **Gemini Life Purpose.** Many are talented – but others are regular people who have a touch of greatness.

Candy Lightner, founder of Mothers Against Drunk Driving, became a public figure to raise awareness and promote tough legislation. She said: *"Death changes us, the living. In the presence of death, we become more aware of life. It can inspire us to decide what really matters."*

Others have had to tackle gender issues – like **Cher,** who is completely womanly, yet embodies female autonomy in a male-dominated industry.

Cher said: *"Women are the real architects of society."*

Sally Field said: *"Motherhood is given the brush-off in our society. 'Oh, I'm just a mom,' you hear women say. 'Just' a mom? Please! Being a mom is everything. It's mentorship, it's inspirational, it's our hope for the future."*

"If mothers ruled the world, there wouldn't be any goddamn wars in the first place."

Both Cher and Sally Field have openly gay children and that inspired them to become activists for transgender rights.

Steven Spielberg built his reputation on *Jaws, Close Encounters*, and "*ET*" but his later movies addressed more serious subjects.

The *Color Purple* and *Schindler's List* gave us an up-close-and-personal look at the tyranny of hate and religious persecution while *Saving Private Ryan* asks questions about the ethics of wartime decisions regarding who is put into harm's way.

Agatha Christie wrote her first detective story on a dare from her sister. It took two weeks to write and the book was rejected by dozens of publishers.

She was painfully shy as a child and heartbroken when at age 11, her much loved father died. Tragedy struck again when her mother died and, the same year – her husband announced that he wanted a divorce. To recover, she took the Orient Express to Baghdad where she met archeologist Max Mallowan.

She said: *"An archaeologist is the best husband a woman can have. The older she gets the more interested he is in her."*

The people who fall short, like Bill Clinton and Arnold Schwarzenegger, are so disappointing because we so wanted them to be great.

Others make us all sad because they've given in to excesses like Charlie Sheen and Amy Winehouse who brought themselves down with drugs, drinking or sex but even then, we judge them gently and forgive them easily.

But those who've found a cause that they believe in and have used their charisma and talent to talk about something bigger than themselves, they become agents for change in a big way and leave a mark on history.

So, the choice is yours, disappointing – or well-loved and celebrated.

These are some of the notables who have found humility and an inner "rightness" of purpose that's instantly recognizable and adds strength to their star power.

Diane von Furstenberg, David Bowie, Elton John, Tom Clancy, David Letterman, Candice Bergen, Gilda Radner, Linda Ronstadt, Suzanne Somers, and Laura Bush.

Charlotte Rampling went from modeling with front covers on *Vogue* and *Elle* to becoming an icon of the sixties with sexually provocative films and nude pictures in Playboy.

On her choice of roles, she said: *"I generally don't make films to entertain people. I choose the parts that challenge me to break through my own barriers. A need to devour, punish, humiliate, or surrender seems to be a primal part of human nature, and it's certainly a big part of sex. To discover what normal means, you have to surf a tide of weirdness."*

WHAT'S NEXT?

- Take time to think about this – until you experience the inner 'knowing' that this is your purpose and true direction.

- Create a circle that engages you in dialog and be patient with them – even though they have a different point of view

- Look at the big picture and don't get stuck in the details or require that everyone agrees with you

- Consider different points of view before you reach a decision about what is "right" and don't keep the disputes and misunderstandings going.

- Notice the things that you're doing right and where you're moving in a good direction.

"Listening is a magnetic and strange thing, a creative force. The friends who listen to us are the ones we move toward. When we are listened to, it creates us, makes us want to unfold and expand."
-- Karl A. Menninger

Chapter 20 – CANCER North Node

"The ache for home lives in all of us.
The safe place where we can go as we are and not be questioned."

-- Maya Angelou

YOUR LIFE PURPOSE – as seen through your Cancer North Node
YOUR GIFTS AND STRENGTHS:

- You are purposeful, sensible, and comfortable being in control.
- You have a deep sense of responsibility.
- You're goal oriented and know how to negotiate a good deal.
- You have good judgment and can make agreements that are fair and honest.
- You're not afraid to take on difficult tasks and you know that what you do will stand the test of time.
- You know that you don't have to outdo anyone and instead, you let your reputation and good work bring recognition.

At work:

- You're patient, disciplined, and quietly deal with limitations.
- You know how to turn theoretical plans into viable projects.
- You instinctively take on a position of influence and can easily see how others can be more productive.
- Others look to you for guidance and they know how committed you are to pursuing goals for the long haul.

Your greatest gift is good judgment, ageless wisdom and insightful humor. You're good at making sense of the business of life and you remember that Churchill said: *"Failure is not final; success is not forever. What counts is getting up and trying again."*

The challenge is that, on a personal level, you often remain stubbornly reserved, aloof, and expect to be treated as an authority figure.

That is challenging for people who are close to you because they can see that you seek recognition from strangers and you're often generous to them, but you have a judgmental attitude towards loved ones and the people who work for you.

Your LIFE PURPOSE

You're the wise one, the law-abiding, authority figure and role model for your community, but to attain your best and highest purpose you must not only embody those qualities but also find a way to be loved, be vulnerable, humble and human.

To get there, let down your guard and allow others to touch you with their emotions.

You're so good at being an influencer in public affairs and perhaps you've come to think that some part of your inner worth is built on this recognition, but to embrace your life purpose, you will need to open your heart and be willing to accept love, affection and attention.

This shift from expecting to accepting may be one of the most difficult things you ever have to do.

Crossing that bridge requires acknowledging and participating, going from standing on the sidelines to actively being involved in the celebration, leaving behind judgment and showing humble appreciation.

Your greatest potential is to create a home environment where everyone can function from a place of non-judgment … a place that's inclusive and where loved ones can feel relaxed and emotionally healthy.

This requires a difficult internal shift. Letting go of any attitude of arrogance, privilege, or entitlement and being generous, humble and human.

You also have to put aside any ideas that you have the right to lay down the rules because, to achieve your life purpose, it's essential that you explore your own feelings… and that means being less in your head and more in your heart.

EARLY LIFE

When you were young, you probably acted older than your years and perhaps you thought it was important to suppress weakness, saying that you were "Ok" even when you were face down in the dirt and hurting.

Perhaps you belonged to a family who took pride in their heritage and maybe thought of themselves as being better than others or having power and influence. Maybe you were taught to judge others as not being 'good enough' if they didn't meet your expectations.

This could have left you with the impression that you had to act dignified and not show any signs of emotional weakness or vulnerability.

Maybe, you sometimes acted out with anger because you weren't in touch with your own feelings of sadness or grief.

Perhaps, even now, you don't want to look like a failure, or let anyone know about your mistakes, problems or inadequacy, so you act like nothing is wrong because you find it difficult to be exposed or vulnerable and you may think that if you had more fame, recognition, or money that others would see you to be the great leader, mentor, and guru you really are.

Thinking this way is not just an attitude. It's become a habit, and it's a difficult one to break but your life purpose is to allow yourself to be loved, for your flaws as well as your strengths.

ACTION STEPS

- Start by not taking yourself so seriously
- Put a "*Live, Laugh, Love*" plaque on your desk.
- Create a home where you feel comfortable, safe, and protected
- Come forward for loved ones and be there when they need a shoulder to cry on or want to vent their frustration.
- Remember birthdays and anniversaries and take time to find just the right card, gift, and words that convey your feelings.
- Acknowledge that sometimes you need assistance, and before you take it to the next level and start blaming others for not being there for you — realize that you've always acted like you didn't need help.
- If you are in a position of authority use your power well. Don't be one of those officious people who are so busy being 'right' that they forget how to be human.
- Don't act as though you're entitled.
- Maintain a childlike wonder.
- Do what you enjoy rather than sticking to a strict routine.

The advantage you have with this life purpose is that people WANT to love, admire and respect you, especially if you are appreciative and humble.

This life-path destiny is said to be 'lucky' but to activate these blessings, you need to do what you love, rather than doing something in order to make money, or to be famous.

"Some people believe that holding on and hanging in there are signs of great strength. However, there are times when it takes much more strength to know when to let go."

--Ann Landers

RELATIONSHIPS

Now it's time to get in touch with your inner source of power, your kind, generous and compassion heart.

Allow others to see you as sensitive and emotionally connected.

Find your inner child and let them out to play, participate, be funny, folksy, friendly and make people feel good.

Realize that loved ones appreciate your good judgment and they're grateful for the financial support but that sometimes it's difficult for them to get close.

With loved ones:

- Go back to your roots to talk about relationships and commitment.
- Consider the legacy and moral values that you want to establish.
- Nurture, cherish, and encourage.
- Be sympathetic to anyone who needs a shoulder to lean on and if there is any divide, release any hard feelings.

Letting go of:

- Withholding love and affection.
- Judging people as "not good enough."
- Sticking to contractual obligations out of a sense of duty but doing it in a way that takes the joy out of work and relationships.

At home

Enjoy the shelter of home and the safety of belonging. Live by water if you can, and if that's not possible, take trips to walk by an ocean, pond, or river and do it because your Cancer North Node is urging you to be emotionally engaged and in the moment instead of living in a world of prestige, social standing and ownership of "stuff."

At work

- Your industrious nature is suited to business. You're good at what you do, and you go the extra mile and take pride in your work.

- You have executive ability and know how to organize.

- You have a natural understanding of how to make a deal and can see where there is a benefit to be gained.

- The negative is that you can see the loopholes and know the weakness in others and sometimes you use that to take advantage of the situation or to be condescending towards people you think are less than your equal.

When working with clients, customers, and employees:

Perhaps you've created a hierarchy in your mind and judged others as frail, weak or undeserving.

That may sound a little harsh and perhaps you're not at that extreme, but the slightest hint of that kind of attitude will create situations where people can't trust you to be fair.

One more problem

You rarely confront the people who frustrate you. Instead, you talk to others about the problem - but never engage and therefore issues don't get resolved.

Don't be impressed by:

Money - followers - degrees - titles.

Do be impressed by:

Generosity - integrity - humility - kindness.

People who share your life purpose:

Michelle Obama, Prince William, Goldie Hawn. With their charisma and social position, they could have been patronizing and condescending but instead they've chosen to be warm, wonderful, and entirely human.

WHO IS STUCK in being condescending towards people? Sarah Huckabee was the Press Secretary for the Trump White House who often belittled the intelligence of journalists.

Worse still and in the "I'm the supreme authority" mode . . . Adolph Hitler.

These are some of the well-known and celebrated people who share your **Cancer Life Purpose:**

Jonny Carson – best known for the *Tonight Show* where he always appeared to be having a casual conversation with his guests.

From the age of twelve, he entertained his family by doing magic tricks and after graduating from high school, hitchhiked to Hollywood where he was arrested and sent home.

Later he joined the Navy, served in WWII, and came back to work in radio and TV.

His late-night show was massively successful, and Jonny made it look easy, but when he went out on stage there was a sign flashing towards the audience that said: "Applaud like crazy."

"On my side," Jonny said, "the sign reads: be humble."

That's the exact message for your Life Purpose: be approachable, be thankful and whenever possible, be funny.

Jonny said: *"Despite the fact that computer speeds are measured in nanoseconds – the smallest interval of time known to man is that which occurs in Manhattan between the traffic signal turning green and the taxi driver behind you blowing his horn."*

Erma Bombeck wrote with ironic humor about her life as a midwestern housewife:

"In general, my children refuse to eat anything that hasn't danced on television."

"It is not until you become a mother that your judgment slowly turns to compassion and understanding."

Mel Brooks –writer, filmmaker and songwriter, known for *Blazing Saddles, The Producers* and *Young Frankenstein.* His father died when he was two years old.

Mel said: *"I may be angry at God, or at the world. And I'm sure a lot of my comedy is based on anger and hostility. Growing up in Williamsburg, I learned to clothe it in comedy to spare myself problems."*

He was small, sickly and bullied by his classmates but found joy when he started performing at age 14, playing piano and drums.

Later he was drafted into the army where he defused land mines during WWII. He said:

"My job is to go out and entertain the most people possible."

In 2014 he was honored with a handprint and footprint ceremony at the TCL Chinese Theatre where he used a prosthetic finger to leave a six-fingered left hand in the concrete sidewalk.

Stephen Colbert — the youngest of 11 children. At age 10, his father and two closest brothers (by age) died in a plane crash. He later described himself as detached and lacking any sense of importance about the things that concerned other children.

To relieve his anxiety and depression, doctors prescribed Xanax and when he quit, Stephen said:

"I'd sometimes hold the bottle, to go like, 'I could stop this feeling if I wanted, but I'm not going to.'"

Later he found that performing on stage gave him the incentive to stay away from prescription medication.

Other much-loved comedians can tell the truth in way that isn't malicious but rather to entertain and share their adult (and somewhat detached view) of a pretentious world.

Harpo Marx, Charlie Chaplin, Harvey Korman, Hank Azaria (*The Simpsons*), and Rob Schneider (*Saturday Night Live*).

Other notables: Mariska Hargitay who plays Detective Olivia Benson in *Law and Order SUV* and Brian Weiss, author of the bestseller *Many Lives, Many Masters*.

Russell Brand said: *"My life is just a series of embarrassing incidents strung together by telling people about those embarrassing incidents."*

Who didn't get the memo and remain aloof and remote:
Rudy Giuliani
Queen Elizabeth II of England
Sarah Palin

WHAT'S NEXT?

- Take time to think about this until you experience the inner 'knowing' that this is your purpose and true direction.

- Surround yourself with people who make you feel safe about expressing the tenderness you feel for loved ones.

- Create a home that you love and share it with your nearest and dearest.

- Be human, have fun, and ask for help and encouragement.

- Notice where having to be the authority figure has cut you off from those who want to love you.

- Recognize that you've done a lot right and that you're moving in a good direction.

"Nearly all men can stand adversity,
but if you want to test a man's character, give him power."

--Abraham Lincoln

Chapter 21 – LEO North Node

"Rule with the heart of a servant. Serve with the heart of a king."
--Bill Johnson

YOUR LIFE PURPOSE – as seen through your Leo North Node
YOUR GIFTS AND STRENGTHS:

- You are the most likable of friends, easy to get along with and aware of how others feel.
- You have integrity, honesty, warmth and generosity.
- You're the mentor that empowers others.
- You accept compliments without letting them go to your head or making you arrogant.
- You understand how to work within the bounds of what is accepted in your community.
- You act in an unselfish, self-sacrificing way and are most comfortable when you are working to achieve public-spirited and altruistic goals.

At work

You want to fit in and defer to the group and that makes you a good employee.

Your greatest potential is to be the guide that shows the way but to do that, you need to be happy, relaxed, and accepting of yourself.

The challenge is that you often don't have the confidence to step forward and say: "I'll take charge of that."

Your LIFE PURPOSE

is to overcome self-doubt and build your inner-strength and confidence so you can spearhead a movement and take a leadership role that empowers others and shows the way for future generations.

This isn't easy for you. You're more comfortable with working with friends to achieve goals, but now you have to take center stage and deliver your message with confidence and enthusiasm.

You may think that you don't have enough education, bravado, or credentials to be a leader, or perhaps you're afraid that a role like that is too intense for you to even contemplate.

The problem is that you have lifetime habits of thinking you're not ready, or not good enough, perhaps that you don't have enough education, or that you need a business degree, more experience, a bigger house, and better shoes.

Maybe you're waiting because you're so entangled on the everyday treadmill that you never look to the bigger vision.

Others see your potential. They see your wisdom and inner strength and they encourage you by telling you that you're destined for great things, but perhaps you doubt yourself and you're fearful of the changes that success could bring.

Your life purpose is to overcome that self-doubt, take a leadership role and do it with humility, knowing that you are working for universal truth, justice, and the evolution of all humankind.

Authentic Leadership is about stepping forward to articulate a visionary message that inspires others to reach for excellence.

Being that kind of trailblazer takes the kind of courage and empathy that begins with a moral center and listens with an open heart because you can't just set out to make money, preserve power, and maintain authority — instead you have to consistently be on the side of ethical behavior and sticking to time-tested values — while giving credit to those who've helped you to create the movement.

EARLY LIFE

During your formative years you probably had experiences that led to submerging your desires. You pitched in, helped out, and rarely said "No" if someone needed your help.

Perhaps you were told that you had to conform and fit in and shouldn't think or act in a way that makes you stand out.

Living like that can cut you off from your dreams and perhaps you were afraid to confront, or you were unwilling to take a stand that would challenge the situation.

Or maybe you never thought of yourself as something special and you're still sitting on the sidelines, afraid that a big wave will pull you in and you'll be out of your depth.

The simple answer is that you don't have to do this alone. You just have to find the right people to support and encourage you — and a cause that you believe in and get involved.

To follow your life purpose, make some intentions around
- Being more assertive
- Working through static situations to break free
- Being a bit eccentric and breaking the mold of what's expected

ACTION STEPS:
- Stand in front of a mirror, look yourself in the eyes, and say "I have the courage to stand up for what is right."
- Practice saying: "I know what needs to be done."
- Look for situations where you act with others for a cause.
- Give yourself permission to not accept any task or project that isn't in your best interest.
- Find an organization where you can watch, learn, and gradually take on responsibilities.

Remember that movements congregate around a leader. You don't have to originate the cause. You just have to find a group that you believe in and join with them to achieve your highest purpose and calling.

Try this when you walk into a room: look around, smile and take a breath, feel your heart opening as you approach, don't lean forwards or be in a hurry, smile slightly, take it all in and allow yourself to be looked at.

Don't be afraid that people are judging you — they are, but they will welcome you if you appear self-assured.

RELATIONSHIPS

You tend to keep your friends a long time and remain intertwined and perhaps mutually dependent, and that's a good thing as long as it isn't at the expense of missing out on your own individual lifestyle.

This is your relationship to-do list:

- Don't be afraid to show emotions
- Relate to childlike qualities and be able to play around and have fun
- Don't wait for more information before taking action
- Enjoy life in the moment without second-guessing yourself
- Be romantic, and don't be shy about showing your feelings, but also allow the other person to have time and space to see the depth of your relationship.

For sure, you don't like fighting, but there are times when working through differences and crunch situations can bring you closer.

You are leaving behind:

Being detached from emotional situations

Being reserved, indifferent, distant and aloof.

Save all that for when you're a leader and need to appear in public.

And remember that life at the top is not the fabled existence that it looks like from the outside – you'll still have to put your pants on one leg at a time.

Another problem is the dichotomy of needing people and yet wanting to be alone, and that may never be resolved.

At work

Perhaps your early experiences led to jobs where you needed to fit into the establishment, be a cog in a bigger wheel, and further the goals of the collective.

You very much want to be accepted and it may be difficult for you to think of yourself as someone who takes charge and organizes others and you don't have to get there immediately, but you do have to adjust your thinking and believe that change is possible.

More likely there will be pivotal moments when you realize that others are looking to you for answers.

ACTION STEPS:

- Find inspiration by reading about the people who've become trailblazing leaders and see how they were also sometimes afraid to step forward.

- Stake out your area of expertise, be generous with your time and look around to see if you can take a leadership position in an organization or committee.

- From there, you can learn how to influence a group: making them comfortable with your leadership while you're learning to take the initiative, and if you're shy or retiring, write a script that presents your ideas, expertise and authority.

- And as you get more comfortable, provide advice, counsel and good judgment, but don't reveal weakness or talk about trauma. That way, you have more mystery and charisma around you, but try to make your projects sound like fun so that others will want to follow.

One more problem

You will probably be tested. Courageous leaders are not accepted overnight. There may be criticism and obstruction along the way.

Don't take that as rejection, but rather that others haven't caught up with seeing the value of what you have to offer.

Key words: vitality, authority, generosity, nobility, self-expressive, commanding, powerful, magnanimous, creative, and dramatic.

You are moving towards:

Serving the greater good.

Sending out a positive message that change can be achieved.

Respecting yourself and being an inspiration to others

Strength doesn't come from winning. It comes from the struggle to win. The striving, toil and adversity, that's what makes your strong.

People who share your life purpose:

President Obama, Jon Stewart, and Princess Diana. They all had your same doubts and reservations and it slowed them down for many years, but eventually they finally stepped forward and found the courage to take on a leadership role.

These are some of the well-known and celebrated people who share your **Leo Life Purpose**

Mahatma Gandhi — used nonviolent civil disobedience to bring independence to India — and with that principle he inspired movements for civil rights and freedom across the world. He believed, said, and proved:

"Strength does not come from physical capacity. It comes from an indomitable will."

Barack Obama is mild-mannered and without ego. He grew up in Hawaii, which offered him the "experience of a variety of cultures in a climate of mutual respect, and that became my world view, and a basis for the values that I hold most dear."

"Change will not come if we wait for some other person, or some other time. We are the ones we've been waiting for. We are the change that we are seeking."

"Change doesn't come from Washington. Change comes to Washington."

There are many writers and comics that hold up a mirror to society and make us smile with their social commentary and you may not think of them as leaders, but they have changed the world.

Jane Austen - she made us smile with her novel *Pride and Prejudice*, which talks about how women had to have an acceptable marriage as the only way to achieve social standing and economic security.

Jane's only education was in subjects that were intended to make her more suitable for catching the attention of a gentleman — needlework, music and French. She said:

"It is a truth universally acknowledged, that a single man in possession of a good fortune, must be in want of a wife."

"There is no charm equal to tenderness of heart."

Famous for being famous, both **Paris Hilton** and **Kim Kardashian** share your Life Purpose… and they were trailblazers for their time.

And — yes, I can hear you saying: "that's not the kind of leader I was born to be," but they had a huge following and they understood the trends, even if it was shopping and an over-the-top lifestyle.

Thankfully, times have changed and now we're focused on more important issues like the environment, equal opportunity, and social justice, but if you want to be a leader, it's necessary to first identify what's important for the time you're living in so that you can use your leadership to right the wrongs.

Princess Diana said that her husband, Prince Charles "*made me feel so inadequate in every possible way, that each time I came up for air he pushed me down again.*"

She eventually overcame her eating disorder and the grief about the divorce and went on to serve the greater good by visiting with sick children as her way of raising awareness for people affected with HIV/AIDS, cancer, and mental illness.

Her best message is perhaps, that:

"*You first need to respect and love yourself before you can become an inspiration to others.*"

Jon Stewart almost single handedly carried *The Daily Show* for sixteen years – making it an alternative source of news for anyone who could see the absurdity of politicians claiming to be supreme leaders.

He was 27 when he first tried stand-up, but it took him a year before he got up the nerve to be on stage. Then for the first two years, he only performed at the 2:00 am show because he didn't have the courage for prime time.

Jon said: "*Insomnia is my greatest inspiration.*"

Others with your Life Purpose: Beyoncé, Justin Timberlake, Jessica Alba, Mick Jagger, Robert De Niro, Jon Bon Jovi, Paul Newman, Alicia Keys, and Margaret Thatcher.

Entertainers who use humor to change people's outlook: Amy Schumer, Steve Carell, Ricky Gervais, and Rosie O'Donnell. Their trailblazing instincts hold up a mirror to what is incongruous and inauthentic in the people who call themselves "top dogs."

WHAT'S NEXT?

- Take time to think about this until you experience the inner 'knowing' that this is your truth, purpose and direction.
- Find a circle that loves, respects and believes in you and allow them to look to you for inspiration and leadership
- Connect to your most heartfelt desires and don't just rely on intellect and logic
- Don't be afraid to love deeply and have it last forever
- Notice that sometimes you think you're not good enough, or don't have the right credentials but please be aware that what's keeping you from achieving your highest goals are the fears that are standing in the way.
- Recognize that you've done a lot right and that you're moving towards being the benevolent and enlightened leader that you are meant to be.

"If your actions inspire others to dream more,
learn more, do more and become more, you are a leader."
— John Quincy Adams

Chapter 22 – VIRGO North Node

"Take care of your body, It's the only place you have to live."

--Jim Rohn

YOUR LIFE PURPOSE as seen through your Virgo North Node
YOUR GIFTS AND STRENGTHS:

- Others trust that you'll do the right thing
- You have high ideals, you're compassionate, and have a vision for all humanity.
- In your personal relationships, you are sensitive, sympathetic and emotionally aware.
- You feel the emotions of others and know when they're hurt.
- Friends and loved ones know that you're loyal, helpful, and sensitive.
- You may have musical or artistic ability, a charismatic personality that is entertaining and captivating, and this, along with your desire to do the right thing, attracts others and makes them want to support you.

At work

You have both the compassion and practical solutions to solve problems.

Your LIFE PURPOSE

From an early age you may have felt that you have a calling to save people, and perhaps the planet, and this mission could be anything from helping the homeless, being an activist, a holistic healer, or providing financial and legal advice to those in need.

Your greatest potential is to be practical, organized, in control and making sure that you provide assistance to people who are worthy of your time and energy.

This element of discrimination is an essential part of your work.

You're not here to save the whole world, but rather to provide the specific tools, advice, and support to help people save themselves.

To get there, you need to be practical, define your goals and understand the detailed work that it will take to implement, and finance your dreams and ideals.

This was difficult in early life and family dynamics may have left you drained, and because you were a sensitive child, you felt the pain and misery of others and you probably chose to zone out into your own world rather than stand up for your own needs and protest.

As a child, this is an understandable reaction but now you need to be in the world and find balance between the ideal life you want to live and the practical functions that make bigger dreams come true.

Your greatest challenge may be that sometimes you allow emotional sensitivities and attachments to get in the way of living a sensible and well-managed life because it's essential that you not only take care of others but also take care of your own physical, mental, and emotional health.

There may some periods of your life where you want to self-medicate, eat too much, or zone out because you're feeling depressed, overwhelmed by the problems and despairing because you can't come up with solutions.

There's also the possibility that you were influenced by lofty ideals or by an authority figure, leader, or the head of your family and that you abandoned reason and only saw what you wanted to see.

You have more potential than any other life purpose, but also more challenges to overcome.

You have high ideals, are honorable and committed to ethical behavior but you may lack the practical leadership, and organizational skills to put these high principles into practice, and, it's not enough to be a far-sighted visionary. You have to bring structure and organization to your plans and come up with a logical, thought-through strategy that's attainable in the "real" world.

That starts with transforming yourself into a vigorous, healthy, and down-to-earth human who takes responsibility for organizing their own time, finances and health.

Not easy. . . and it doesn't take superhuman powers, but it does require determination, strength of will, and self-control.

EARLY LIFE

When you were young, you thought your parents were like everyone else, until you figured out that your way of life was at the extreme ends of the spectrum, either hazy, confused and out of step — or subject to rules that dictated your daily habits, but didn't always have your best interests at heart.

You may have seen suffering and being the sensitive, wanting-to-do-good child, you avoided adding to their pain.

Even now, those feelings are close to the surface and you often feel drained by the interaction.

It's not wrong to feel deeply or to want to reach out and help, but the problem is that in the reaching, you lose yourself.

When you were young, you may have disregarded your own needs in order to satisfy others. You followed the rules and measured success by other people's standards, but to achieve your life purpose, you may have let go of the ideas you grew up with and be pro-active about taking care of your own priorities.

You could START BY making some intentions around:
- Being less fearful that something will go wrong and that you'll make mistakes that can't be put right.
- Overcome anxiety by doing one thing at a time and being focused and methodical.
- Have confidence in your abilities and know that you can solve problems.
- Notice where you feel the stress in your body.
- Have a plan, crack the code and have answers, because that will make you feel more confident.

Do all that… without losing your creative and visionary ideas for making the world into a more compassionate, honest, and decent place to live.

ACTION STEPS

- Practice being fully present and mindful.
- Observe your physical body and be aware of stress. Awareness is the first step in keeping track and that will help you to see recurring problems.
- Notice when you feel the need to escape, avoid, and evade and notice if there are occasions, or people who particularly provoke this response.
- Look for holistic ways to take care of your health.
- Notice the ways that you like to escape – by binge-watching TV, using drugs or alcohol, losing yourself in work, feeling like a victim or being depressed and withdrawn.
- Tackle this tendency to escape by creating a routine of everyday habits and small rituals that keep you on track.

Know that what happened cannot be changed, but you can come to terms with it and give yourself credit for being older and wiser now.

Allow for the possibility of a different outcome if the same event were to happen again.

- Find stability and fulfillment in an orderly daily schedule
- Clear away clutter and find clarity
- Develop your personal talents and gifts
- Live a discriminating lifestyle that values self-control over giving authority to others
- Set and maintain boundaries to compartmentalize different areas of life.

Letting go of:

- Blind trust and uncritical devotion to a person, corporation, social movement or family values.
- Getting so caught up in a single idea or cause that you're no longer being discriminating.
- Using your head (not your heart and guts) to frequently reassess the situation.
- Being dependent on anything that contributes to an unhealthy lifestyle.

RELATIONSHIPS

You're coming from a place that gives loving devotion from the heart and your capacity to love is so strong that you feel uneasy when you see the hurt of loved ones. You very much want them to be happy and carefree so you try figure out what it will take to make them feel better.

The problem is that sometimes you go through the motions, but others sense that you're doing it by the book rather than being fully present and that separates you, rather than bringing you together.

What they want is for you to be present and do from the heart not from a sense of duty or because you have a plan to make them happy.

That's not easy.

At work, you know what's the ethical thing to do and you have no trouble doing it - but when it comes to family and loved ones, you to tend to either comply or zone out.

Being dutiful and doing what's "expected" in an intimate situation can damage the relationship.

At work

Find situations where you can stay focused by helping others and giving service, and not just the big issues: but also, the day-to-day business of life — like staying on top of budgets and getting the best deal for your cell phone.

You're here to help and be of service and, if dealing with the details sounds tedious and mind numbing, it is, but when you concentrate on the small stuff and maintain an orderly work routine, it not only pays off in performance for yourself, but also creates dedicated followers that want to hear your message.

Your Health is very important and you need to show that you're fit, strong, vigorous and a role model that expresses strength of mind and body because that's your way of showing that the highest principles of calm enlightenment can be manifested through good health and longevity.

People who share your life purpose:

George Clooney, Bernie Sanders, and Tony Robbins.

Perhaps, like Tony Robbins, you have answers for personal success and abundance or, like Bernie Sanders you want to influence public policy.

Many have heartbreaking stories of early life but it's never the depth of despair that defines your Life Purpose, it's the ability to turn around, use the knowledge and create a life that's successful, fulfilling, healthy, vigorous, and helping others to achieve their highest potential.

You have big ideas but to make them work, you have to give attention to rigorous implementation.

These are some of the well-known and celebrated people who share your **Virgo North Node** Life Purpose.

Many suffered through tragic childhood drama and personal pain, but they turned adversity to advantage and appear to the public as gracious and charming.

Tony Robbins is known for his motivational seminars, YouTube videos, and the personal coaching style. His programs have helped millions of people overcome emotional trauma and go on to peak performance.

His describes his early home life as chaotic and abusive. His mother chased him out of the house with a knife when he was 17 and Tony never returned. He supported himself by working as a janitor and did not attend college and, by being successful, Tony has turned his hardship into an inspirational journey that helps others to overcome. Now his charity programs are in more than 2,000 schools and 700 prisons.

He said: *"Quality questions create a quality life. Successful people ask better questions, and as a result, they get better answers."*

Cary Grant – was an only child after his mother lapsed into depression following the loss of his brother.

His father (who'd secretly had a son with another woman), told Archie that his mother had gone away on a "long holiday" and it was only when he was in his thirties that Cary Grant discovered that his mother was still alive and institutionalized.

Maria Callas was known for her love affair with Aristotle Onassis and her diva temperament. The truth is that she was courageous, bold and talented. Maria moved beyond her wartime childhood issues and went on, after dramatic weight loss in middle age, to re-invent herself as glamorous and desirable.

She is still one of classical music's best-selling vocalists.

Marlon Brando - in his autobiography, *Songs My Mother Taught Me*, said: "*The anguish that her drinking produced was that she preferred getting drunk to caring for us.*"

Of his father, he wrote: "*Nothing I did ever pleased or even interested him. He had a habit of telling me I would never amount to anything.*"

Christian Dior – despite international acclaim, his private life was bleak, full of sadness and anxiety.

He was discreetly gay, but after several failed love affairs with younger men, Dior told friends that he felt ugly and repulsive. The private angst didn't show, and friends never outed him, but the fashion icon never had a comfortable home life or satisfying personal relationship. He said:

"*Make me a perfume that smells like love.*"

"*A country, a style, or an epoch, is interesting only for the ideas behind it.*"

John F. Kennedy Jr. – surely had a most heartrending childhood. He lost his father to an assassin's bullet when he was three years old, his uncle five years later and his mother when she moved the family to live on a Greek private island to marry Aristotle Onassis. John Junior was quoted as saying that he considered his stepfather "a joke."

Bernie Sanders – shows how devotion to a single cause (even a good one) needs to be reassessed sometimes.

He is the longest-serving independent in US political history and despite being a visionary, his commitment to the "Medicare for All" with no exceptions has cost him support in the Democratic primary.

Some of the heartthrobs that share the Virgo North Node: George Clooney, Hugh Grant, Paul McCartney, Harrison Ford, Sean Penn, Jean-Claude Van Damme, Antonio Banderas, Colin Firth – and surely the world's most unlikely leading man: Stephen Hawking.

Hawking said: "*I have noticed even people who claim everything is predestined, and that we can do nothing to change it, look before they cross the road.*"

"*We are just an advanced breed of monkeys on a minor planet of a very average star. But we can understand the Universe. That makes us something very special.*"

Others who share your life purpose: Kate Hudson, Kobe Bryant, Dennis Rodman, Rue Paul, Martin Scorsese, Michael J Fox, Charlton Heston, Julian Moore. Eddie Murphy, RuPaul, Michael Fox, Charles Dickens.

WHAT'S NEXT?

- Take time to think about this until you experience the inner 'knowing' that this is your authentic truth and purpose
- Find friends who appreciate your practical, analytical, and organizing skills
- Be modest and be of service by finding clarity of purpose
- Do that by sorting through the chaos and finding the good intentions behind the confusion
- Notice the habitual thinking patterns that have kept you from achieving your goals
- Notice where you've been part of the problem instead of all of the solution
- Hang on to your visionary ideals but don't get so stuck on one far-seeing idea that you reject other possible solutions
- Go for it – the world needs you to be present.

"Things work out best for those who make the best of how things work out"
--John Wooden

Chapter 23 – LIBRA North Node

"There are two basic motivating forces: fear and love.
When we are afraid, we pull back from life. When we love, we open to all
that life has to offer with passion, excitement, and acceptance."
--John Lennon

YOUR LIFE PURPOSE as seen through your Libra North Node
YOUR GIFTS AND STRENGTHS

- You have high energy with pioneering, leadership qualities
- You willingly trail blaze new areas of business and professional performance
- You're not afraid to be seen, or be part of a performance
- You have a competitive drive and an innovative attitude
- You have the inner resources and the courage to survive in difficult circumstances
- You have presence and the stamina to initiate a strong point of view
- You want to be acknowledged for your contribution, even though at times you find yourself in situations where others get the credit and the spotlight.
- You've learned to make fast decisions and take action, to protect your self-interests and fight off the competition, which has most likely put you into a management position at work.

That and your healthy sense of self-identity has made you a role model perhaps to the point where others see you as iconic and want to emulate your achievements, but when it extends into your private life, that same attitude can leave you isolated.

Your LIFE PURPOSE

is to achieve a balance between being totally autonomous and alone or merged into well-adjusted relationships.

To get there, you need to find an inner clarity about yourself and your needs, and ask if you want to be self-sufficient, functioning and effective, or if you are willing to accept comfort, support, love, and encouragement while still being independent. And, if you decide to foster equal and committed relationships in your personal, and working life, how will you put boundaries in place.

Your Life Purpose is to be open to the idea of having shared goals and, as you develop empathy for others, to become aware of your own needs and emotional reactions.

To get there, you will need to allow others to see you as emotionally vulnerable and less protective of your distinctive individuality, knowing that you are precious and have much to give but that you're also willing to receive.

In business or your professional life, look for associates that have collaborative opportunities or joint resources. Build a team and be the leader that empowers everyone by giving credibility to those who teach, help and mentor.

As you build your team, don't talk about winners and losers, instead, show how working as a team will bring results and please remember that it's not just about meeting obligations, you must also leave time for romance and social get-togethers.

To achieve that, do not isolate yourself – be energized, be inclusive and add grace by giving compliments and small gifts.

EARLY LIFE

Experiences may have included harsh discipline, a significant change in family circumstances and/or events that seemed at the time, to be arbitrary.

Perhaps you saw these incidents as messing up your life and frustrating your desire to move ahead with your plans. Perhaps you were rebellious at home while being a good student or the other way around.

Either way, you found it difficult to compromise or negotiate. You wanted to fight, run away or do anything just so that you could get on with your life plan, but the truth is that this was not something that pulled you off track, instead these situations challenged you to deal with people in a more cautious way.

Early in life you had few choices and perhaps those encounters left you with little-or-no self-esteem in some area of your life but as an adult, you can decide to do better and I sincerely hope that you'll choose to hold on to your individuality while creating healthy partnerships and win-win situations.

RELATIONSHIPS

Perhaps there was an early marriage, unwanted pregnancy, or difficult people that made you pull (or push) away maybe thinking that if you could only fix 'them' - that it would solve the problem.

You've probably closed yourself off to the idea of a loving relationship and perhaps it's hard to trust after all you've been through, but no matter how much pain and darkness you're carrying, you deserve to be loved and valued just for yourself.

You're allowed to have wants and needs. It's not a sign of weakness and doesn't mean that you're a failure. It just means that you have a heart and soul and that you're human and not destined to go it alone.

This is at the heart of your Life Purpose and this is a pivotal, watershed moment when you realize it's not weakness to want to be less alone and that you can find a balance between total self-sufficiency and having to submerge yourself in a relationship and be dependent.

Indeed, you could think of that as being pro-active about self-care but as you reach out, look at who deserves your trust and has your highest good and welfare in mind.

It's human to want to have a friend, but don't assume that everyone around you is trustworthy.

It's important to have an understanding of who's on the other side of the contract because when you know better, you do better... but all the while remember that your vulnerability is a precious gift to be shared.

It's important to be discriminating about who you reveal yourself to and, if that sounds negative, you could think of it as a way to filter both the people that you're presently surrounding yourself with and the ones you meet as you make progress towards your highest and best Life Purpose.

Romantic relationships can be especially difficult. You long for a soul mate to share your dream.

But, as you've discovered, too often you attract people who have great potential, but they need your devotion and strength, and maybe it's difficult for you to give up your dreams in order to support theirs.

Perhaps they don't have self-discipline, courage, determination, or strong self-identity and when you see their frailty and flaws, you might turn away thinking that you don't have time for them because you have your own itinerary to follow – but that would again leave you isolated.

ACTION STEPS - and this is not going to be easy

- Be comforting and encourage others to talk about their needs and find a middle ground that recognizes and accepts that they are exceptional in different ways.
- Create equal and honest relationships
- Allow others to talk about feelings without thinking that there has to be a solution to the issues.
- Learn to express your feelings in a tactful, diplomatic way.
- Validate the feelings of others
- Ask how you can be helpful at family gatherings – and don't talk about your work or your latest project but instead promote togetherness and say: "let's get back to the reason we're all gathered here for this special event."

Key words to remember are harmony, companionship, balance, charm, grace, social activities, justice, fair outcome, intelligence, emotional fulfillment, popularity, approval, initiating community activities and interests.

Give thanks for: stability, beautiful possessions, art, clothing, luxury and civilized living.

Please remember that **relationships** may feel like they're real and solid, but they actually only exist in the world of feelings, and while that can develop into a commitment structure, the threads that connect you are still nebulous.

Know that you can bridge the gap between what's invisible and what's solid by naming the feelings (however brief and passing) because naming things brings them into a material place.

With this in mind, give some thought into how to make the invisible more conscious so that you feel more powerful.

There is power in naming things, especially emotional stuff.

Letting go of:

Going to extremes, unbridled passion (for a cause or idea)

Feeling like you're not getting enough approval

Promoting your vision at home when you should be enjoying the closeness of family time

At work

- To achieve your Life Purpose goals, you need to think of your work and business as a team-sport and get good players to work on your projects.

- Pull in any help you need and partner with others even if that feels uncomfortable at first.

- Get clear on your financial, energetic and emotional ties.

- Do your best to see disagreements coming and work them out, but on the other hand, don't be run over by those that need attention, control or have to work out their childhood issues on you.

- Look for relationships with those who aren't afraid to keep it real and to that end, speak up about what you value most but do it in a diplomatic way.

- Be around people who appreciate your gifts, notice and give back approval.

- Make decisions that are in the best interest of the group.

- Ask questions and be aware of how others see you.

ACTION STEPS

Learning to

- Harmonize
- Synchronize
- Co-ordinate
- Co-operate

- Work as part of a team
- Be the coach, counselor, and the one who is uplifting and encouraging.
- Calmly respond to criticism.

Be around people from every walk of life, listen and engage. Learn from their experiences and do this because when you confine yourself, you define yourself and then it's difficult to get back on track.

Be happy and content. That doesn't mean letting go of goals and cherished dreams, it means acknowledging that this is where you join with others to achieve goals and to achieve harmony and balance.

People who share your life purpose:

John Lennon, Madonna, and Michael Jackson. Their star qualities gave them the opportunity to perform and be seen as unique, but in their private lives, they struggled with marriage.

Emmanuel Macron, Prince Phillip, and Nancy Reagan. They all achieved remarkable harmony in their relationships and used that compatibility to show the world that a good partnership completes them and doesn't take away from their individuality.

These are some of the other well-known and celebrated people who share your **Libra North Node** and Life Purpose. You have charisma, you're authentic, pioneering, and mysterious and that's attractive and exciting but your independent nature makes relationships a challenge.

Tina Turner is known for her long career and the heartbreaking story of love that turned abusive when she wanted to become a solo performer.

Since then, her own passionate voice and legendary stage presence has made her the Queen of Rock 'n Roll and she has sold more than 200 million records worldwide.

Tina was raised a Baptist in Tennessee but became a Buddhist and credits the mantra chants with giving her the courage and tenacity to get through the domestic abuse and difficult divorce from Ike.

She said: *"When it came to role models, I looked at presidents' wives. But if I'd been that kind of person, do you think I could sing with the emotions I do? You sing with those emotions because you've had pain in your heart."*

Shakira was rejected in school for the choir because her music teacher told her that she "sounded like a goat."

Despite this, she released her first record at age 13, which did well on the Columbian radio.

Her fourth album sold 10 million copies worldwide and at age 22, she won her first Grammy.

Unfortunately, Shakira's personal life has not been easy. Her first romantic relationship was with an Argentine lawyer who managed her business, but she terminated that after 11 years and started a romance with a football player who plays for Barcelona in Spain. He is ten years younger and they two children, but they have not married.

Bob Hope did vaudeville, Broadway, radio, television and movies and was honored for entertaining US armed forces. He died at 100, joking to the last, in the hospital he said: "I'm so old, they've canceled my blood type".

Raquel Welch – *Men's Health* magazine rated her as #2 in their list of *Hottest Women of All Time* and for *Playboy* she was #3.

Raquel was married four times and has now stated that she does not intend to do it again.

In the 1960's her image was of a torrid sex temptress, but private life was quite different. She said: *"Privately, I dislike any hoopla. It's not my nature to be a sex symbol and the fact that I became one is probably the loveliest, most glamorous and fortunate misunderstanding."*

Madonna – at age six, her mother died from breast cancer leaving six children to be cared for by their father. When he married their housekeeper, and had two children, Madonna became rebellious at home, while in school being a cheerleader and straight 'A' student.

She was awarded a dance scholarship in Michigan, but dropped out, preferring to work at Dunkin' Donuts in Manhattan while she took classes and tried out for dance troupes.

Her marriage to Sean Penn broke up when she started spending all her time with Sandra Bernhard, which she later confirmed was an affair.

She continued to shock, and in 1993, embarked on *The Girlie Show World Tour*, in which she dressed as a whip-cracking dominatrix surrounded by topless dancers.

Anaïs Nin – born February 21, 1903, Neuilly, France – author, famous for her journals and erotica. She wrote: *Each friend represents a world in us, a world not possibly born until they arrive, and it is only by this meeting that a new world is born.*

Others who share your Life Purpose:

Michael Jackson, John Lennon, Bruce Lee, Ashton Kutcher, Isaac Newton, Simon Cowell, Kevin Spacey, Michelangelo, Judy Garland, Thomas Edison, Joan Crawford and Jamie Lee Curtis.

WHAT'S NEXT?

- Take time to think about this - until you experience the inner 'knowing' that this is your truth and purpose
- Don't isolate yourself. Look for a circle of people who encourage you to be socially active and engaged
- Be open to lasting relationships
- Notice that when you reject people who offer partnership and belonging, that you lose a part of you that wants to be loved and understood
- Create beauty and harmony in your home and let that be your launch pad for making the rest of the world more agreeable
- Recognize that you've done a lot right and that you're moving in a good direction.

"We don't see things as they are, we see them as we are."

-- Anaïs Nin

Chapter 24 – SCORPIO North Node

"When we set exciting, worth-while goals for ourselves,
they work in two ways: we work on them, and they work on us."
--Bob Moawad

YOUR LIFE PURPOSE – as seen through your Scorpio North Node
YOUR GIFTS AND STRENGTHS

- You are resolute, single-minded and focused
- Can create stability in crisis situations
- You empower others
- You're an expert in banking, insurance and securities and know how to create financial resources by saving and investing
- You're an investigator or researcher who uncovers motives and makes sense of what is ambiguous and uncertain
- You step in and take charge when others don't know how to handle their finances or are not being sensible about their priorities.

Your LIFE PURPOSE

is to overcome inertia and let go of any tendency to stay put. To get there, you may have to go through some serious changes in your living situation, let go of something you've been hanging onto that is a source of security and be fearless about taking the next step.

This is no easy path. The standard way of life is being attached to comfort while accumulating possessions, but you have to break the mold, overcome stagnation and let go of a predictable routine.

You may already have a personality that's not afraid to push through barriers and shatter glass ceilings and perhaps that has already created transformational changes in your life but you may also find yourself tested and changes forced on you by circumstances, like a marriage break-up, or a work situation that became so tedious that you have to escape.

These changes would be difficult for anyone, but in order to feel fully alive, you've had to find your passion and perhaps jump into high-risk situations.

This is a core issue for you because your life purpose is to be a true and inspiring leader, a social change-maker and front-runner for radical new beliefs. Lasting success is yours when you're willing to let go of what is conventional and solid and embrace the energy of transformation

Fortunately, you're living at a time when transformative changes are already in the air and when you tune into that wave of energy, it makes you feel alive and excited.

EARLY LIFE

Most likely the formative years were difficult for you. You valued stability, predictability and security and while you very much wanted your domestic and family life to continue unchanged, there were probably events that turned your existence upside down.

These experiences left you feeling anxious and maybe you buried the emotional reactions and appeared to be stoic.

Even as an adult, you like to feel the solid earth under your feet and if there's upheaval, you resist and would prefer to remain steadfast in a job or relationship, even if you feel increasingly restricted and depressed.

These disruptive events were actually giving you the courage to confront issues, to investigate your inner reactions and know that you can survive.

Change doesn't have to be bad. In fact, when you embrace new situations, you may find that you come back better than before and knowing that helps you go from someone who is anxious, to someone who can embrace the opportunity to pursue a new course.

At work

Look for dynamic situations where you help others to change, especially if you can help them see the bigger picture by going through the self-discovery and/or therapeutic process.

You are evolving towards:

- Being aware enough to let go of the old habits and choosing to be an agent for positive change.
- Eliminating possessions that no longer serve a useful purpose
- Being able to enjoy nature and beautiful things without having to own them
- Accepting new ideas, opportunities, and allowing yourself to be supported by others both emotionally and financially.

You could **START BY**:

- Knowing that you're doing the right thing and that it's a part of your Life Purpose to move on - even if that means you have to step into unknown territory.
- Being aware of the situations where you're safe but that don't offer you room for growth
- Seeing how important it is that you feel intensely passionate about your work.
- Taking time off to travel to new places so that you can re-discover what's important to you.

ACTION STEPS:

- Know that you're creating the future with the steps that you take today.
- Have the courage to take on new situations, even though sometimes you feel stressed out and anxious.
- Assign more weight to your needs and give yourself permission to take chances and make changes.

Starting today see where you're stuck and do it because self-understanding is the most precious gift you can give yourself. When you get to the authentic bedrock of who you are, you'll also figure out where you're giving away your power.

To get there, find adventures and experiences that are transformative even if they seem a little scary.

Perhaps, this all sounds extreme and a little dangerous and for sure, it won't be easy to let go of your routine habits and make groundbreaking changes, but in your heart, you know that remaining in the same predictable circumstances will suffocate your spirit.

For you, it's important to put your precious destiny in your own hands.

"The two most important days of your life are the day you were born and the day you find out why."

--Mark Twain

At work you have practical solutions and are good at creating win/win situations.

Your greatest potential is to use your talent, gifts and strengths in the service of others – to be the kind of leader that gets out of the way and makes the group think that they did it by themselves.

You're good at:

- Making decisions for the group's best interests
- Sharing unconventional ideas
- Creating win/win situations
- Finding dynamic situations where you can help others to change

You need an occupation where there are problems to solve and where you can find a resolution that's inclusive, fair and progressive.

It's your calling to take this on and you do it because the world needs your progressive ideas, and without your vision, we're all in a bad place – so, if you wake up on a Monday dreading going to work or the highlight of your week is Friday, or pay-day – know that you need to make changes.

Yes… it's difficult to walk away. It's a scary idea, but for you, the real challenge is staying where you are because that will eventually affect your health and wellbeing.

Instead, you need work with like-minded people and to function within a group, because you have to go where you're appreciated, know your worth and be aware of your destiny as a visionary and change-maker.

Start by taking baby steps towards something that you can feel passionate about.

- Find a circle of like-minded people where you can talk about your vision.
- Network, volunteer, and look for classes and organizations where you can learn new skills.
- Look for a Facebook group of people who are on a similar journey.

You deserve to live a life of adventure and while it's not always easy for you to work in a group — the paradox is that when you do, you're most likely to be recognized.

You already have the power and strength of a superstar and now it's time to be uplifting to others.

The challenge for you is that you sometimes become so fixed on the outcome that you forget to allow others to have goals and follow their dreams.

RELATIONSHIPS

can be difficult, and you may sometimes have to put aside time to deal with your own inner turmoil.

Do your best to forgive and let go even though it might be the most difficult thing you ever have to do. Trust that these experiences are there to learn from and so that you can turn your pain and grief into something positive that can help others.

ACTION STEPS

You need to engage, listen, and help people to recognize the value of their dreams and intentions, especially since this creates a window for you to continue to re-evaluate your own goals.

Your LIFE PURPOSE isn't an easy one.

It requires that you find fulfillment in working for the greater good.

At times you will have to accept criticism, to be the outsider, the trailblazer and the frontrunner because being the agent for change isn't always comfortable and often brings resistance from those who are being asked to make space for a new way of doing things. But, if you're willing to take on this challenge, you can advance the growth of all humankind, while finding success, recognition, and financial freedom for yourself.

You may have to give up the work and career situation that you've built, and you go through some scary times in order to be transformed into a more powerful version of yourself.

Most people never find the courage, but with your life purpose, you don't really have a choice because if you remain too long in a place, you may find that changes are forced on you and you'll have to find a new marriage partner or a different direction in your career.

People who share your life purpose have gone through similar challenges:

Ellen DeGeneres, Walt Disney (who had four failed businesses before he made it big) and Abraham Lincoln who took a leap of faith and made a historic difference.

These are some of the well-known and celebrated people who share your **Scorpio Life Purpose:**

They are the courageous pioneers who have moved the world forwards by venturing out beyond what is conventional and having the audacity to do something courageous.

Ellen DeGeneres came out as a lesbian and after that, she didn't work for two years.

Charles Darwin found the courage to publish his book: 'Origin of the Species'.

President Lincoln went from small town country lawyer to President of the United States because he wanted to stir up public opinion against slavery.

They all knew that it would be an uphill battle and were willing to defy convention and take on the criticism.

Katie Couric was co-host of the *Today* show and could have remained there safe and much loved, but instead, she left to become the first woman anchor of CBS evening news.

Her iconic interview with Sarah Palin was spoofed by *Saturday Night Live* and heralded as the most significant negative influence in the McCain campaign.

Couric made it look easy but in her long career, Katie went through many situations where the rug was pulled out from under her and others where she created the upheaval out of her own determination to move beyond what was static and stodgy.

It's that unusual mixture of pioneering energy coming together with the sweetness of her demeanor that has kept her followers engaged.

Coco Channel created casual chic and liberated women from the constraints of the "corseted silhouette" and she did it using cotton jersey, which until then had only been used in the manufacture of men's underwear.

Coco's early life was a bleak existence of poverty and strict discipline.

At age 12, her father sent her to an orphanage because her mother died and it was there that she learned to sew and make rag dolls – but rather than bringing her down, the harsh conditions fueled Coco's determination to achieve outstanding success.

To get there, she had to go though many transformations, first working as a nightclub performer, then designing hats and finally as a boutique owner selling luxury clothing for sports and leisurewear.

Her brand still flourishes, and her name sells her distinctive perfume as well as her pocketbooks and eyeglasses.

Steve Harvey hosts an afternoon show plus a game show, and he is the author of: *Act Like a Lady, Think like a Man.*

His father was a coal miner and his Mom stayed home. Harvey first performed standup comedy when he was 28 and for several years was homeless, sleeping in his ten-year-old Ford when not performing at gigs that provided a hotel. His extended family helped him out with a contract for carpet cleaning and credit at a travel agency.

Harvey says that his third wife changed his life and made him a better man. He is a born-again Christian and advises women not to have relationships with atheists, whom he calls "idiots".

His on-air personality is fearless, hospitable and optimistic, but behind the scenes, Steve is relentless and ambitious. He has seven children and three of them are stepchildren.

Ron White's blue-collar humor gets him in trouble – yet he adds to the problem by mouthing off… as demonstrated by his bestselling book: *"I Had the Right to Remain Silent but I Didn't Have the Ability."*

Derek Jacobi seems to play both sides of the fence. He mesmerized audiences in *"I, Claudius"* with his TV performance as the stuttering monarch – but in his private life, Jacobi avoids confrontations and awkward situations by leaving the room.

Colin Farrell turned his life around when he overcame his addiction to painkillers and recreational drugs and after coming out of rehab, he spoke about it on the *Late Show with David Letterman.*

He has given support to the anti-bullying campaign, "Stand Up" which is an Irish LGBTQ youth group and has become the Ambassador for the Homeless World Cup, which uses street football to inspire homeless people to change their lives.

Bernie Madoff is the poster child for what happens when you don't make the transition from money-based consciousness to pursuing a higher Life purpose.

Others who share your Scorpio North Node: Copernicus, Walt Disney, Daniel Day Lewis, Tiger Woods, Gary Oldman (big acting style), Carrie Fisher, Reese Witherspoon, Natalie Wood, Alec Baldwin, Fran Drescher, Clark Gable, Blake Sheldon, Louis Armstrong, Fellini, Francis Ford Coppolla, and Ted Turner

And Marlene Dietrich who said: *"It's not the legs darling, it's what you do with them."*

WHAT'S NEXT?

- Take time to think about this until you experience the inner 'knowing' that this is your truth and purpose
- Find a circle of friends who appreciate your passionate way of being
- Look for work and projects that give you the freedom to explore – and use that passionate energy to manifest what you want
- Be the investigator that explores the mysterious.
- Notice where you've remained stuck, perhaps because you need a financial safety net, but also know that you have the power to fly, soar, and learn the way of the eagle.
- Recognize that you've done a lot right and that you're moving in a good direction.

*"Nobody can go back and make a new beginning,
but anyone can start today and make a new ending."*

--Maria Robinson

Chapter 25 – SAGITTARIUS North Node

"There are three constants in life . . . change, choice and principles."
--Stephen Covey

YOUR LIFE PURPOSE as seen through your Sagittarius North Node
YOUR GIFTS AND STRENGTHS

- You have many fine qualities. You sense other people's point of view and instinctively know what to say to get your point across.
- You easily make friends with co-workers, neighbors and just about anyone you meet.
- You are curious, like to investigate and can make sense of the world through logic, reason and language.
- You enjoy a spectrum of intellectual discussions.
- You easily assimilate new ideas and especially like to talk about travel, philosophy and enlightened concepts.
- You find diversity interesting and enjoy meeting people from every walk of life.
- You are inspiring, optimistic and uplifting to others.
- You act as a catalyst for others to meet.
- You love to keep busy and are always asking questions and researching for answers.

Your LIFE PURPOSE

is to find that quiet, inner, tranquility and reach for wisdom and higher universal truth – but you must first find your own peace of mind.

That may sound easy but for you it's been a problem, because being with people energizes you and keeps you motivated.

You've learned to fit in, to work with others, become a gifted communicator and perhaps a consummate salesperson, teacher or marketer.

These skills are in demand and well paid but that way of life doesn't always bring you satisfaction, joy, or recognition and happiness may never be available through worldly accomplishment or a bigger paycheck because what pleases you the most is being in nature and being in the moment with a simple ritual or routine.

Your Life Purpose, however, is to move in the direction of peace and tranquility because that's what supports and inspires you and as you learn, you teach others about values, and the simple integrity of being in the moment and avoiding the mind chatter.

Learning this brings joy and excitement to you, inspires others and helps you find your authentic purpose.

And please be aware that your wisdom is much needed now as humankind makes a transition towards a greater and higher truth.

EARLY LIFE

You had many friends, lived in an urban community and enjoyed the adventure of places to go and people to meet.

If there were problems at home, you were more likely to escape than to stay and witness the suffering of loved ones. That was the right thing for you to do and helped you to keep your balance.

When it came to spirituality, a sense of balance was not so easy to find. At home you probably saw one of two extremes: either that religion was strictly observed - or you came from a background where parents had differing beliefs but managed to co-exist.

This may have resulted in being at the far ends of the spectrum, either strong convictions and dogmatic or being willing to change your opinion to fit the situation.

As for education, you were ambivalent about college and higher education, preferring to learn from life experiences and books.

If you went to college, you found distractions, friendships and social events that tended to pull you away from being a serious academic.

You enjoyed sports, engaged in social activities and preferred working on your own projects to the strict regimen of classes and academic life.

Bill Gates, who shares your Life Purpose, was a college drop-out.

He preferred working with computers to going to class. And like him, perhaps you saw that you had gifts and skills that would make money and depending on other factors in the chart, you may have turned into an over-achiever and put all your energy into business at the cost of having a personal life. Later, when Bill Gates saw the good that money can do, he said: *"As we look ahead into the next century, leaders will be those who empower others."*

Or you may prefer a lifestyle that's a bit unconventional, using your ability to persuade and "sell," to support an entrepreneurial business, or to think about the bigger and more universal issues of society today.

RELATIONSHIPS

You like having strong family ties and in order to keep loved ones close, you're willing to see their point of view, but this can make it more difficult for you to make strong stand-out statements or voice your doubts about the status quo.

Perhaps you married at a young age and started a family and that didn't allow you to be alone, or go on adventures, which may have left you frustrated, impulsive and inconsistent.

It's possible that you've experienced the pain of infidelity, or been involved in a love triangle of some kind,

This can bring up disputes over money and difficulties with distant relatives.

All this may have created conflict earlier in your life, but when you found your soul mate, that person encouraged you to think more deeply into your more philosophical side, helped you to find center and encouraged you to reach for a more Zen-like existence.

With a good partner and maturing into your own philosophy, you come to value animals, have reverence for nature and find a peaceful wisdom in your own back yard.

At work

- You instinctively know what is popular and commercially viable.
- You know how deal with the public.
- You learn quickly and communicate facts and ideas easily. Your words have a powerful effect, and this gives you an edge with sales, marketing and influencing others in your circle.

- In business, your confidence in an idea or project makes it easy to convince others of the value and with this skill, you easily promote and expand into new areas. If you sell, write or teach, you easily find new markets and clients.

These are the gifts that help you find a good job or career and you may find success in sales, marketing, public relations or anything to do with writing, publishing, teaching or entertainment but be aware that bigger fame and fortune is not likely to bring greater peace of mind and that's what you're really after.

CHALLENGE – you like to keep busy and if your mind isn't thinking about your next work project, you're planning a trip, or figuring out what's next on your to-do list.

The issue is that you find it difficult to draw a line between work and play and that can easily turn into a workaholic attitude that keeps you toiling away, being prolific and high functioning, when what you need is to spend time just being, breathing and enjoying.

This 'being busy' is a difficult habit to break but you could ease yourself away from the need to be productive by finding an activity that is rhythmic and repetitive in nature and let your hands do the work, while you guide your thoughts towards mindful and conscious awareness of the moment.

As your mind adjusts to being somewhere between motion and stillness, you could fall in love with the joy of being you and knowing that you are fulfilling your life purpose just by the simple appreciation of this precious moment.

ACTION STEPS:

- Be still and find time for introspection, either in solitude or peacefully with your soul mate and partner.
- Learn about different religions and see the philosophical and spiritual principals that transcend the dogma.
- Find the inner compass that guides you towards ethical behavior.
- You may want to travel to learn about other cultures, or you might look for a different kind of adventure by reading and understanding great minds.

- The challenge is always to find yourself and understand that you are part of the connected universe.

CHALLENGES – you're a team player and you know how to play fair, but your idea of integrity doesn't always line up with what the law-and-order magistrate says is justice and sometimes your idea of what's right corresponds to a higher order.

Just know that at those times, you need to speak your truth, protest the inequalities and bring your wisdom down from the mountain to help those who are struggling.

People who share your life purpose – and we don't think of them as super stars, but rather as people with a big message:

Tom Hanks, Pope Francis, Jackie Robinson, and Henry Ford.

Like them, you can contribute, teach, inspire, and embolden the world to look for truth and a bigger purpose.

These are some of the well-known and celebrated people who share your **Sagittarius Life Purpose** and it's their values, humanity, and lack of ego that makes them significant.

Henry Ford didn't invent the automobile, or the assembly line and it was not his engineering skills that made the difference, it was his business philosophy:

"A business that makes nothing but money is a poor business."

"Coming together is a beginning; keeping together is progress; working together is success."

"If I had asked people what they wanted, they would have said 'faster horses.'"

Ford attracted the best workers by paying twice as much as his competitors – believing that when people lived well, they would want to buy a car, and that it would benefit his business and the larger economy.

Henry left most of his money to the Ford Foundation to do philanthropic work around the world.

Jackie Robinson made his Major League debut with the Brooklyn Dodgers, and that ended eighty years of racial segregation in baseball and while he was well supported by the sports media, there was tension in the clubhouse, as well as rough play, ridicule, and shouts of racial slurs from fans and opposing teams.

Martin Luther King, Jr. said that Jackie was *"a legend and a symbol in his own time,"* and that he *"challenged the dark skies of intolerance."*

Friedrich Nietzsche was a German philosopher, cultural critic, writer, and poet. He questioned everything: morality, power, religion, concepts of good and evil, and education. He said:

"The surest way to corrupt a youth is to instruct him to hold in higher esteem those who think alike than those who think differently."

"That which does not kill us makes us stronger."

"He who has a why to live for can bear almost any how."

Franklin D. Roosevelt led the United States through the Great Depression and World War II.

He was shaped by family values and the Episcopal boarding school where the headmaster urged his students to enter public service. He said:

"The only thing we have to fear is fear itself."

"Remember, remember always, that all of us are descended from immigrants and revolutionists."

"There are many ways of going forward, but only one way of standing still."

A. A. Milne – is known for his Winnie the Pooh books.

He said: *"Pay attention to where you're going because without meaning, you might get nowhere."*

"What day is it?"

"It's today," squeaked Piglet.

"My favorite day," said Pooh.

His genius is most alive in the restrained attitude of his "toy" characters, like the philosophical Winnie-the-Pooh who reminds us to live and love in the moment.

Other who share your life purpose are fearless leaders and pioneers who are often ahead of their time but always act with courage and speak their minds: Chelsea Handler, Whoopi Goldberg, Bill Maher, Leonardo DiCaprio, Harry Styles, Miley Cyrus, Nelson Mandela, Russell Brand, Kris Jenner, Jane Fonda, Antony Hopkins, Jimmy Fallon, Morgan Freeman, Ernest Hemingway, Swami Vivekananda and George Washington.

WHAT'S NEXT?

- Take time to think about this until you experience the inner 'knowing' that this is your truth and purpose
- Find a circle of people who appreciate your wisdom and support your inspirational ideas
- Acknowledge that you haven't always been a good role model but that when you connect to nature and find your inspiration you acquire understanding and good judgment
- Know that you've done a lot right and that you've learned to practice mindfulness and being in the moment

"Labor to keep alive that little spark of celestial fire called conscience."
— George Washington

Chapter 26 – CAPRICORN North Node

"What is to give light must endure burning."

--Victor Frankl

YOUR LIFE PURPOSE as seen through your Capricorn North Node
YOUR GIFTS AND STRENGTHS

- Empathic listening
- Child-like wonder
- Sense of fun
- Wanting to please and astonish people
- Most of the time you're forgiving, patient, and thoughtful
- You know how to overcome limitations, dejection and melancholy
- You ask questions and are good at finding creative solutions that have universal appeal.
- You nurture, cherish, and encourage loved ones.
- You make friends, share ideas, and connect with your community.

At work:

- You encourage everyone, mentor and treat people like family.
- You're concerned about safety measures, guarantees, and security.
- You make people feel comfortable by talking about relationships and commitment, and you're sympathetic to anyone who needs a shoulder to cry on.
- You're a specialist in your home market.

Your LIFE PURPOSE

is to stand up, shout out, and be noticed

You dream big and you're ambitious. You know in your heart that you can be successful in business and that you have the drive and skills to turn visionary ideas into concrete reality, and while it's easy for you to set high goals, getting there has been a problem.

You easily become absorbed in the emotional needs of others and may feel like it's your responsibility to help them deal with their issues.

People come to you for a shoulder to cry on and a hand-up, but when it comes to expressing your own needs, they expect you to be strong and put aside your problems to deal with their hardships.

This can become a constant drain on your time and resources, but there is always an inner knowing that you have goals to accomplish and to get there, you need to be less generous with your time, grab the spotlight for yourself and speak out.

The time is now.

This is a pivotal time in human history. We need your maturity and your heart-centered, accountability – and we need you to show up and bring your power, purpose, and energy to reach across obstructions and break through glass ceilings.

We need you to succeed.

Not just for yourself, but also to make space for others to follow.

Please do this because, when you're on purpose, you bring resolute energy that is:

- Focused
- Practical
- Organized

This is all good, but for you, it's not enough to just achieve.

You are that rare combination of down-to-earth sensible and future oriented visionary – and you have to build world-class accomplishment and recognition.

EARLY LIFE

Maybe you started life with not-so-good role models.

You may have had problems with one or both parents who were not supportive and tried to make you into something you're not.

Perhaps you were born into a family situation where dysfunctional family members took the reins and you were a by-stander.

Or maybe you heard that you were not good enough, didn't measure up to their standards, or maybe, like Oprah, you were an unwelcome child. (Yes, she has your life purpose).

This could have left you feeling powerless and may have left you feeling emotionally drained.

You may have tried to take responsibility even to the point of thinking that it was your job to get your family back on track, and that may have become part of your personality.

All of this is challenging because your Life Purpose is to strike out on your own and the hurtful criticism may have left you without the self-esteem and emotional resources to take charge.

ACTION STEPS:

Getting beyond thinking you should be the perfect parent and trying to live up to that, or expecting your own parents to embody the quality of unconditional love.

Notice when you feel neglected, unloved or guilty about putting your needs ahead of family because this holds you back from putting your focus on the priorities of your lifetime purpose.

BABY STEPS

It's always been difficult for you to deal with emotional situations. Perhaps you cry at a sad movie, or when you see a child, or animal in trouble and that part is fine but to achieve your dreams, you need to be in control, not so much that you never cry or feel happy but with enough self-restraint that it doesn't escalate and take over your ability to think and reason.

TAKE ACTION:

- Keep your eye on the prize and learn from miss-steps and mistakes.
- You don't have to be great to do your life purpose, but you do have to build a circle of influence.
- In your marriage partnership you may not get a white-picket-fence kind of domestic situation and at times you may have to put aside your goals or get help to fulfill family obligations.

- There may be times when you'll be criticized but you know that you have to be brave and daring for the sake of progress.
- Looking back, you may see that being safe is not enough and that you need to create a bigger, brighter future for yourself.

RELATIONSHIPS

can be the most difficult part of your Life Purpose journey and for that reason, success may come later in life, after you've fulfilled obligations towards family and loved ones.

Or you may find that you can do both when you delegate and get help.

Remember:

"Success is not final; failure is not fatal: it is the courage to continue that counts." – Winston Churchill

Prioritize your goals and focus on what will generate results.

Don't get caught up in a flood of 'have-to' details.

- Talk to people who are experienced but also look for the people who challenge you.
- Address objections, and not from the ego but after you've done the research and are sure of your facts. This will make your case stronger.
- Start local and build from there.
- Learn to present your ideas in writing and in person in a compelling and visionary way.
- Take time out to relax and heal from the stress that you're putting yourself through because it's during the quiet times that you are in touch with your inner purpose and authentic self.

At work:

It may be difficult for you to decide exactly what you want to do, or who you want to become.

The truth is that you don't need to know. The marketplace will tell you and all you have to do is listen, but you do need to find something that you can be successful at and take the first step, put yourself out there and not be afraid to succeed or fail.

- Make your business enterprises popular and commercially viable

- Understand what it takes to be successful and keep bringing new ideas to your working environment
- Build strong foundations for a successful enterprise by getting help from experts.
- Express your personal power through wise business decisions
- Have patience for the long term
- Keep quiet about the challenges while making your accomplishments look easy
- Commit to your vision and let your reputation and good work bring recognition.
- Be sincere and stable in your affections and allow others to help you succeed
- Empower others
- Learn to deal with experts, organizations, and red tape.
- Put in whatever effort is necessary to make it happen but also find time to relax and restore the inner clarity.

ACTION STEPS

- Put your goals first.
- Get used to the idea that you can be a leader and authority figure.
- Know that your goals are within reached, and that those are milestones on a bigger journey
- Get past the 'needing to belong' syndrome and create your own tribe.

Maintain a routine and/or spiritual practice that can calm the mind and use that as a way to deal with work pressures that cause stress.

Be patient and disciplined in dealing with limitations.

Bring good judgment to the table, honor traditions, find the inner satisfaction that comes from doing a good job – but also find inspiration for a higher, better and more evolved spiritual connection.

Key Words: organization, ambition, accomplishment, show integrity, conserve assets, capacity for hard work, troubleshooting, acquire knowledge of practical affairs, and sensible use of assets.

People who share your Life Purpose:

Oprah, Heidi Klum, Leonardo Di Vinci, and John Travolta. They didn't have college degrees or business experience, but they found mentors and supportive collaborators to help.

This will also be true for you because, once you start, there will be people who will see your strength, determination and talent.

Your life purpose and higher calling is your source of your power and when you're going in the right direction, nothing can stop you.

These are some of the well-known and celebrated people who share your **Capricorn Life Purpose.** Some had to be pushed, others were impelled by outside circumstances, but they were all great when they spoke out for peace, progress, and commitment to evolution of spirit.

John F. Kennedy was privileged and educated in the best private schools. He never had political aspirations until his father urged him to run for office.

JFK supported public housing, civil rights, immigration, and labor unions and he asked profound questions:

"If not us — who? If not now — when?"

His average approval rating of 70% is the highest of any president in the Gallup poll's history and when he said: *"We choose to go to the moon in this decade and do the other things, **not because they are easy,** but because they are hard,"* we all knew that it was to challenge people to come up with the technology, not as a way to grab attention for himself.

The 14ᵗʰ Dalai Lama was taken — at the age of two, along with his farming family, to begin a monastic life where he was educated in poetry, drama, astrology, and Buddhist spiritual tradition.

This peaceful existence came to an end in 1950 when he was driven out of Tibet and had to flee to into exile in Northern India and, despite the challenges, he consistently advocates policies of non-violence, even in the face of extreme aggression.

"If you think you are too small to make a difference, try sleeping with a mosquito."

"Every day, I think as I wake up, today I am fortunate to be alive, I have a precious human life, I am not going to waste it. I am going to use all my energies to develop myself, to expand my heart out to others; to achieve enlightenment for the benefit of all beings."

Leonardo Da Vinci was an artist, inventor, engineer, sculptor and painter.

He dissected corpses to learn about anatomy and in his notebooks, drew prototypes of an airplane, submarine, and a helicopter.

He was the son of a wealthy notary and a peasant mother and was stigmatized for his illegitimate birth. As a teenager, he joined his dad in Florence but was barred from joining guilds that would have led him into a conventional career.

Instead he became Europe's most celebrated sculptor and painter and is still known for his "Mona Lisa," for futuristic ideas, and for the engineering principles that he applied to body structure.

He said: *"Knowing is not enough; we must apply. Being willing is not enough; we must do."*

Steve Jobs – passion pours through him and his laser-like focus is on the thing in his hands as that is the identity he presents to the world.

He is a hero, a leader and a visionary but there was another side because when he was young (in his thirties), Steve Jobs was not so agreeable. His employees were afraid when they saw him coming and his critical remarks could bring them to tears.

Oprah Winfrey

"I don't think of myself as a poor deprived ghetto girl who made good. I think of myself as somebody who from an early age knew I was responsible for myself, and I had to make good."

"I still have my feet on the ground, I just wear better shoes."

We applaud their accomplishments and all the more because they are decent, honest people who didn't set out to become celebrities, they just did the best they could and they struggled, but when they started to achieve, they pulled out all the stops and went for the gold.

Other who share your life purpose are leaders and pioneers: John McCain, Jerry Seinfeld, Lena Horn, Jude Law, Notorious B.I.G., Pavarotti, Christopher Columbus, Yves Saint Laurent, and Pharrell Williams (Happy).

Of course, not everyone with Capricorn North Node is a positive role model and some fail to reach their goals while others used their power and position in a bad way.

But if you choose to use this energy to organize the people that you mentor, know that sometimes, it's OK to push them to do better, be better, and go for big goals.

WHAT'S NEXT?

- Take time to think about this until you experience the inner 'knowing' that this is your truth and destiny
- Find the talent, authenticity, and commitment to reach for the highest and best for yourself and for all of humanity
- Create a circle that listens and recognizes you as the disciplined, responsible person that holds it all together
- Notice that when you allow others to set the agenda that you're limited by their expectations
- Know that you've done a lot right and are now ready to step forward and be the authority figure, spiritual leader, and enlightened role model that others look to

"Things do not happen. Things are made to happen."
--John F. Kennedy

Chapter 27 – AQUARIUS North Node

"We make a living by what we get, but we make a life by what we give."
--Winston Churchill

YOUR LIFE PURPOSE – as seen through your Aquarius North Node
YOUR GIFTS AND STRENGTHS

- You treat people with dignity and rarely get angry
- You know that with sensible planning, you can get through a crisis – and not just survive but thrive and move on with gratitude and forgiveness.
- You learn quickly, you say profound things, and you have an inner knowing that you need to accomplish something meaningful.
- You find original and progressive solutions to problems that confound others
- You can see what's in the group's best interest and make decisions that move everyone forward
- You're future oriented and can see how things need to change
- You can have intense emotional experiences but you're rarely uninterested and would prefer to be passionate than jaded and bored.
- You're the champion and advocate for humanitarian causes, but at times your commanding personality can be a bit too dramatic.

At your best, you know that human dignity and civil rights are not luxuries for people and countries that have a high standard of living, but a necessity for all humans.

Your LIFE PURPOSE

is to make your voice heard and talk about your progressive, humanitarian ideas.

Eastern religions would say that you're an old soul that's returned to help move the world towards an enlightened future by shifting towards a more compassionate attitude.

To get there, you must engage your powerful will and creative gifts by either working through or creating organizations that motivate others to take action – but you're not meant to go it alone.

You will need to motivate others to take action and yes, you could do it better, faster, and more efficiently by taking over and getting things "done," but that's not the goal.

You're the catalyst that's here to help people evolve to the point where they can work together and believe that they did it by themselves.

This is not an easy life path.

You have to let go of any feelings of entitlement and this is difficult because your reputation is important to you and you want to be taken seriously, but this is not about you.

It's about creating a movement that has a lasting effect.

Sometimes this frustrates you because there's a lingering issue of wanting to set the rules because, darn it... it would be so much better if you could just carry out your mission and everyone would just follow your guiding light.

In the end however, you need to take a step back, work through the collective, and use your warmth, charisma and influence to bring people together in alliances where they can work together for a cause.

EARLY LIFE

There were experiences that brought attention to intellectual capacity, or your musical, creative and artistic talent.

Perhaps you were charismatic, had presence, and showed leadership qualities that set you apart.

You knew that you didn't quite fit into the mold of typical or ordinary but instead of bringing pleasure, this left you feeling somewhat isolated and all the more because, despite your intelligence and talent, your wishes and needs were often ignored, perhaps for a family drama.

Perhaps you had to deal with a divorce, or one parent missing, either physically not there, emotionally absent, or because their workload took them away.

You wanted to give practical assistance but also knew that if you got in too deep you would take on more than your share of responsibility.

There may even have been a watershed moment when you had to choose between drama and turmoil or continue your education and life-path in a more tranquil environment.

RELATIONSHIPS

These early-life challenges put an emphasis on developing your intellect and creative talents and, knowing that you had a mission to fulfill, you put energy into a sensible, purpose-driven education so that you would be in a good position to give back.

This is helpful for business and professional success, but your commitment to humanitarian ideals and having odd friendships may have put you outside the norm of family obligations and that, along with your ideas of how others should act, and your disappointment when others didn't live up to an ideal, made you somewhat fearful of commitment.

This feeling of being slightly separated from loved ones can sometimes make you feel exasperated, moody and negative towards them, especially if you keep your frustrations to yourself.

This tends to push you towards being more involved in groups and friendships and the determination to pursue freedom and the strong inclination towards philanthropic goals is your Life Purpose, and at this time in history, it's important that you work through your personal challenges and get on board.

At work

You have practical solutions and are good at creating win-win situations.

Your greatest potential is to use your talents, gifts, and strengths in the service of those who are less fortunate and to help people realize the benefit of treating people and animals with dignity and respect.

To achieve these goals, you need to provide the kind of visionary leadership that gets out of the way and makes the group think that they did it by themselves.

You are fortunate:

- To have the resources that help those who are needy
- To know people who are social activists, kindred spirits and have group activities that connect you to a bigger cause.
- To have a more evolved social consciousness and you're probably on the leading edge of a movement that will take humanity towards a better destination.

You're good at:

- Making decisions for the group's best interests
- Sharing unconventional ideas
- Creating positive outcomes.

This attitude makes you good in any career or business but to be fully satisfied you need an occupation that inspires you, where service to humanity is imbued in your work and you can find solutions that are inclusive, fair and progressive.

It's your calling to take this on as the world needs your enlightened ideas in the next decade – especially since you can work with like-minded people and function in a group without needing public recognition just for your own ego.

The challenge is that you have the power and strengths of a superstar and it's not easy for you to back off and submerge those qualities, and still trust in a positive outcome. The paradox is, that when you do, your ideas are most likely to be recognized

On the other hand, it's better that you don't become so fixed on the outcome that you forget to allow others to follow their dreams.

Friendships are important and can bring much happiness.

ACTION STEPS:

You're working towards looking for a higher vision.

Reach out to as many people as you can to put focus on the big issues, like inequality, climate change, an end to war, famine, addiction and poverty, and doall this with humility, not being afraid to be well-loved and popular but not allowing that to be your main objective.

Write and say these INTENTIONS:

- I easily make friends and I'm comfortable with group endeavors
- I am open to new, stimulating, and inspiring ideas
- I quickly gain an understanding of business and professional strategies
- I am comfortable with technology
- I align myself with community and humanitarian causes
- I easily balance my male and female energies

Please do not give up even if you're impatient with how slowly the world is moving towards that vision. Always believe in a positive outcome and know that your frustration can be a force that will move issues forward.

We are living through a revolutionary time when old thinking can be replaced with new ideas and original concepts.

People who share your Life Purpose:

These are some of the well-known and celebrated people who share your **Aquarius Life Purpose.** They tend to be quiet individuals who work to engage others as they grow their concerns for humanity into a movement that makes a difference.

Jane Goodall spent 55 years in Tanzania studying the social and family interactions of chimps and gorillas. She said: *"You aren't going to save the world on your own. But you might inspire a generation of kids to save it for all of us."*

She now serves on the board of the Nonhuman Rights program and in 2002 was named a UN Messenger of Peace. She believes, like so many others, that: *"The greatest danger to our future is apathy."*

Like her, your life purpose is concerned with groups, causes and movements where people are talking about society's problems, injustice, and the need for collective action. The problems are big but, if you can add your individual voice to a cause, you can make a difference.

John Lennon – singer, songwriter, and peace activist. When he was critical of the Vietnam War, and the Nixon administration tried to deport him. He said: *"When you do something noble and beautiful and nobody notices, do not be sad. For the sun every morning is a beautiful spectacle and yet most of the audience still sleeps."*

Marianne Williamson — writer, speaker, and democratic Presidential candidate offers a different approach to spirituality that encompasses Eastern, Christian and Judaic wisdom. She says:

"Your playing small doesn't serve the world. There's nothing enlightened about shrinking so that other people won't feel insecure around you. We are all meant to shine, as children do. We were born to make manifest the glory of God that is within us. It's not just in some of us; it's in everyone. And as we let our own light shine, we unconsciously give other people permission to do the same. As we're liberated from our own fear, our presence automatically liberates others."

Gloria Steinem was first recognized as a leader and spokeswoman for the feminist movement in the 1960's and 70's. She was a columnist for *New York* magazine and co-founder of *Ms.* Magazine. She said:

"A woman without a man is like a fish without a bicycle."

"A liberated woman is one who has sex before marriage and a job after."

Your personal challenge: sadly, some people with your passion and aspirations get pulled off center. They're unhappy, even though the world sees them as successful.

Brigitte Bardot — after a movie career made her famous as a sex symbol, she became an activist for animals. She said:

"I gave my beauty and my youth to men. I am going to give my wisdom and experience to animals."

Bardot was born to a wealthy family, went to ballet lessons, private school, and vacationed on the Riviera.

Her first husband said that: *"She didn't get much affection from her parents and when we started dating, she didn't want jewels, but a dog."*

She married four times, and her last husband said that it was an accident when she overdosed on pills and cut her wrists.

Others who share your Life Purpose and passion: Elon Musk, Larry King, Louis Pastor, Shaquille O'Neal, Claude Monet, Caroline Myss, and Kathie Lee Gifford.

WHAT'S NEXT?

- Take time to think about this until you experience that inner 'knowing' that this is your calling and purpose
- Recognize that you're on the leading edge of a movement
- Surround yourself with peace-loving, like-minded, people who appreciate you for being unusual, unconventional, and authentically yourself
- Notice where you're still hoping to be a leader, and see that when you aspire in that direction, it slows you down.
- See that you've already done a lot right and that by being a unique role model you're inspiring to others.

"The first problem for all of us, both men and women,
is not to learn, but to unlearn."

--Gloria Steinem

Chapter 28 – PISCES North Node

"Since everyone is an individual, nobody can be you.
You are unique. No one can tell you how to use your time.
It is yours. Your life is your own. You mold it. You make it."

- -Eleanor Roosevelt

YOUR LIFE PURPOSE – as seen through your Pisces North Node
YOUR GIFTS AND STRENGTHS:

- You can easily analyze situations and make sense of work systems and routines.
- You look at problems from several different viewpoints and figure out what needs to be done.
- You understand where you belong in an organization and you fit into a hierarchy.
- You have a sense of what it will take to restore order.
- You come up with targeted answers.
- You identify with the work you do and the service you give – and you take responsibility for what goes wrong.

Your LIFE PURPOSE

You've always had an inner understanding that you are here to rescue, protect, and serve.

You have a big heart and want to help the innocent, liberate the oppressed and find ethical solutions for the world's biggest problems – but to fulfill your highest purpose, you need to help one person at a time and do it without judgment or worrying about who deserves to be healed and who doesn't.

Doing this makes you a visionary and a healer, but to present your enlightened point of view, you need to talk about your ideas in a way that's creative, exciting, and entertaining ... and I mean that in the broader sense of the word: that you make people stop, pay attention and be mindful.

This is a big job. An overwhelming job and you can't do alone. You need help and sometimes that puts you into a panic because you believe that people could die, evil may win, and atrocities be committed.

This is difficult because you've always been something of an expert at fixing things and you're methodical, organized, practical, and have experience in situations where knowledge and expertise solves the problem.

Now you are faced with issues that are not so easily solved, where suffering and misery can't be helped with practical consideration or medical answers, where "just do it" isn't enough, and only compassion and emotional support can ease the suffering.

This is a difficult shift to make, and to do so your life purpose must lift others through tenderness, empathy and concern and you may have to learn that these unseen vibrations are real and you have to trust and be guided by your gut feelings, more so than by your knowledge and expertise.

To get there, you may need to pay attention to spiritual realms and look to organizations that bring growth, compassion, healing, and fulfillment by serving others.

EARLY LIFE

Most likely your life was either chaotic, or it was structured, with too many strict rules, and not much middle ground.

Maybe you saw both ends of the spectrum with one parent carefully maintaining order and the other restless, ambiguous or just plain out-of-touch.

Either way, these early experiences left you feeling that you needed to create structure.

Perhaps your answer was to have a strategy to take care of the details with rules and a plan to follow, or perhaps you assigned that job to someone else, a loved one, or an administrator at work so that you could feel more relaxed.

In the end, this need to control leads to more tension. Even when everything looks calm and is running on schedule, you're still somewhat afraid that something could go wrong.

Perhaps as an adult, you still think that your well-ordered life could turn into a chaotic mess, that rules might be broken and circumstances could sweep you away and all this adds up to worry, stress and anxiety.

Even if your early years were not so extreme and you had more middle-of-the-road parents, these inner fears are still with you and at some point, you need to understand these issues, because if you can't help yourself, you surely can't help others who are less fortunate.

Mostly likely you had some gifts and talents that set you apart and those in authority wanted you to learn and concentrate on mundane tasks that needed to be done correctly.

This may have set up a pattern of being both rebellious and stubborn, which often stops you from using your best skills and strengths to advantage.

Many of these issues go away when you find meaningful work, doors open, and positive emotional energy becomes available to you.

When you feel stressed, let music be a part of your journey and especially gospel, praise and worship, (or whatever is best tuned in to your needs).

Create a home or work environment that's healing, meditative, natural, with bells and other ambient sounds.

RELATIONSHIPS

Your mixture of idealist sensibilities and the need for structure makes it difficult for you to be with a partner who doesn't live up to your highest expectations.

You long for a transcendent love, but when it comes to everyday domestic situations, you want someone who supports your lifestyle and understands your devotion to a cause.

This is more difficult if you have "star" qualities and don't want to share the spotlight because you may unconsciously push away anyone who might compete.

If this is a recurring pattern, look at your inner stress factors and especially any fear of being alone.

Lighten up, get help, and realize that while you're a part of the problem: you're 100% of the solution.

THINGS TO DO in relationships:

Share your passion. Talk about the big ideas, spend time with like-minded people and let positive ideas flow into your life.

- Be friends first
- Talk about your values and be with people who have high ethical and moral standards
- Encourage others to talk about their needs and try to listen without passing judgment regarding whether they are worthy of getting your help.

Letting go of:

- Feeling responsible and thinking that it's your duty to remain and give service.
- Excessive worry
- Feeling anxious about making mistakes
- Getting stressed out over details and worrying about what you're not.

Your parents, siblings, and friends are already proud of you. Feel their joy and breathe in their attitude.

Do what you do best and feel sustained by a message of hope.

Awareness first and when you know better, you do better.

Work and Career goals

For you, it's not just finding the right work, you need to feel connected and have a vocation where being of service to others can be imbued into your work.

Buddha said: "*Thousands of candles can be lighted from a single candle, and the life of the candle will not be shortened.*"

You are that candle. You are the energy and power that can light others with your vision, music, and ability to make people laugh and when you use those gifts to support a cause, you can make a difference.

In Eastern religions, they would say that you are a soul that has returned with the intention of dedicating yourself to bringing awareness.

Whether you believe in past lives or not, you know in your heart that you are here for a purpose and when you do it well, you remind us that the greatest strength is in compassion and kindness.

Be aware of your finances. Wanting to do good for others doesn't mean you have to live poor. Neither is it an excuse for being overconfident about money and getting into debt.

ACTION STEPS:

- Trust in a positive outcome and be uplifting to others
- Talk about the big picture, rather than judging or thinking that you have the one and only solution.
- Give practical help, but also allow others to choose whether they want to be whole or broken.
- Take time for reflection and mindfulness, because when you come from a place of peace and serenity, you radiate that and that attracts the right people to support and encourage you.

If this sounds tedious and mind numbing it is — but big aspirations require intentional practice.

- Make a pledge to overcome any deeply rooted fears or feelings of not being good enough.
- Rescue yourself as well as others
- Overcome any guilty feelings about not doing enough
- It's not how many hours you spend working, it's what you're working on that matters.

At work:

- Avoid any work that requires you to focus too heavily on details.
- Have your private space where you can be organized.
- See if you can include a connection to water, the environment, ocean biology, water distribution or treatment.
- Align yourself with non-profit and charitable causes.
- Use your creative writing or musical skills as a way to talk about social issues.

People who share your Life Purpose:

Some people with your life purpose say that they got help from Divine intervention, from psychic sources or messages

People like Nostradamus, Joan of Arc, Edgar Cayce, and John Edward (the TV personality who communicates with spirits).

Others are healers: Dr. Phil has a TV show that talks about mental health issues and helps his guests with substance abuse, past trauma and relationship issues.

Some of them look as if they're here to entertain, but they have a deeper and more profound message that gives hope, heals, restores, and takes care of people, animals and the environment.

These are some of the well-known and celebrated people who share your **Pisces Life Purpose.**

Many of them serve the greater good by being healers and leaders and they relate through music, laughter, and art by using the restorative energy of unconditional love that gives without judging who deserves to be helped – or resentment if their message isn't heard.

This Life Purpose brings a diversity of paths and outcomes, from the most mystical, to those in entertainment who grab our attention so that we can be in the moment.

In entertainment:

Jennifer Lopez, Carole Burnett, Tina Fay, Renee Zellweger, Robin Williams, Gwen Stefani, Joan Rivers, Elizabeth Taylor and Babe Ruth.

There are also the people who bring healing and spirit messages from another realm like: Nostradamus, Joan of Arc, and Edgar Cayce.

A few bridge the gap between the arts, writing, and performance, like **Jonny Cash.** His best-known songs were "I Walk the Line" and "Folsom Prison Blues" which were recorded live at a concert for the prisoners of the California State prison. Cash said that he always wore black on behalf of the poor and hungry and for prisoners who've long paid for their crime.

He said: *"The old are neglected, the poor are poor, the young are still dying before their time – and we're not making many moves to make things right."*

At age five, Cash started working in cotton fields, singing along with his family. At age twelve, his brother Jack was pulled into a whirling saw machine at the mill where he worked and was almost cut in two. He suffered for over a week before he died.

Jonny wrote in his autobiography that he felt guilty because despite his own and his mother's premonitions of danger, his brother insisted on going to work as the family needed the money.

Jonny and his wife June Carter toured together for 35 years until her death.

At his last concert, Cash read a statement that he had written before taking the stage: *"Her spirit overshadows me tonight with the love she had for me and the love I have for her. We connect somewhere between here and heaven. She came down for a short visit, I guess, from heaven to visit with me tonight to give me courage and inspiration like she always has."*

He died four months later.

Charles Baudelaire — was known for his essays and poetry and when others were writing lyrical verse about the pleasures of nature and rural living, he celebrated hedonism, decadence and sensuality.

"Poetry will be born of our intimate union. We shall create together and soar heavenward like sunbeams, perfume, butterflies, and all winged things."

He spoke of heaven but smoked opium, drank to excess and suffered a massive stroke that left him paralyzed a year before his death at age 45.

Dr. Phil combines the desire to help people with a practical philosophy that says:

"We teach people how to treat us."
"You can't change what you don't acknowledge."

WHAT'S NEXT?

- Take time to think about this — until you experience the inner 'knowing' that this is your truth and purpose
- Realize that some things can't be explained by reason and logic and there's a whole realm of enlightenment to be explored
- Surround yourself with people who live their higher purpose
- Know that you are the healer that serves without judgment
- Acknowledge that in the past, you wanted to do good, but you haven't always achieved that noble and exalted ideal.
- Recognize that you've done a lot right and that you are an inspiration to others

"You can't change what you don't acknowledge."

--Dr. Phil

APPENDIX

Look up the year you were born,

and then read your chapter.

APPENDIX

To find your Life Purpose sign, just look for the year you were born and read that chapter.

1932 –until January 6:	Chapter 17
1932 - January 7 – to end of year	Chapter 20
1933 –January I to July 25	Chapter 28
1933 - July 26 to end of year	Chapter 27
1934 – All year	Chapter 27
1935 – January I to February 12	Chapter 27
1935 - from February 13 to end of year	Chapter 26
1936 – January I to August 31	Chapter 26
1936 – Sept I to end of year	Chapter 25
1937 – All year	Chapter 25
1938 – January I to March 21	Chapter 25
1938 – March 22 to end of year	Chapter 24
1939 – January I to October 8	Chapter 24
1939 – October 9 to end of year	Chapter 23
1940 – All year	Chapter 23
1941 –January I to April 27	Chapter 23
1941 – April 28 to end of year	Chapter 22
1942 – January I to November 14	Chapter 22
1942 – November 15 to end of year	Chapter 21
1943 – All year	Chapter 21
1944 – January I to June 3	Chapter 21
1944 – June 4 to end of year	Chapter 20
1945 – January I to December 21	Chapter 20
1945 - December 22 to end of year	Chapter 19
1946 – All year	Chapter 19

1967 – August 20, to end of year	Chapter 17
1968 – All year	Chapter 17
1969 – January 1 to April 19	Chapter 17
1969 – April 20 to end of year	Chapter 28
1970 – January 1 to November 2	Chapter 28
1970 – November 3 to end of year	Chapter 27
1971 – All year	Chapter 27
1972 – January 1 to April 27	Chapter 27
1972 – April 28, to end of year	Chapter 26
1973 – January 1 to October 26	Chapter 26
1973 – October 27 to end of year	Chapter 25
1974 – All year	Chapter 25
1975 – January 1 to June 9	Chapter 25
1975 – June 10 to end of year	Chapter 24
1976 – All year	Chapter 24
1977 – January 1 to January 7	Chapter 24
1977 – January 8 to end of year	Chapter 23
1978 – January 1 to July 5	Chapter 23
1978 – July 6 to end of year	Chapter 22
1979 – All year	Chapter 22
1980 – January 1 to January 5	Chapter 22
1980 – January 6 to the end of year	Chapter 21
1981 – January 1 to September 24	Chapter 21
1981 – September 25 to end of year	Chapter 20
1982 – All year	Chapter 20
1983 – January 1 to March 15	Chapter 20
1983 – March 16 to the end of year	Chapter 19
1984 – January 1 to September 11	Chapter 19
1984 – September 12 to the end of year	Chapter 18
1985 – All year	Chapter 18
1986 – January 1 to April 5	Chapter 18
1986 – April 6 to end of year	Chapter 17
1987 – January 1 to December 2	Chapter 17
1987 – December 3 to end of year	Chapter 28
1988 – All year	Chapter 28

Story of an Astrologer

"If I had more time, I would have made it shorter."

--Ernest Hemingway

Eastern traditions say that it takes more than one lifetime to learn the heavenly arts and that would explain how the first five years was a series of "ah-huh" moments of remembering, rather than learning new material.

Book after book, I absorbed complicated manuals as easily as lighthearted novels, yet despite years of study, teacher after teacher, doing calculations and memorizing aspects, I was still doing "cookbook astrology."

To improve my skills, I began doing readings in psychic circles, spending the evening surrounded by the intuitive readers who were lighting candles, chanting prayers and shuffling tarot cards.

Some had a following that would line up, waiting for answers from the cards that were spread across the table as they listened intently to the psychic who would say in a profound voice: *"I can see that you..."*

The less popular ones (like me) would sit and wait.

On slow nights, I exchanged readings and saw how Tarot cards could describe current events and circumstances, but when looking into the future, too often I heard stories of love, money and wish fulfillment — and when asked to give a timeline, some psychics would say: *"In five weeks, five months, or five years."*

Astrology, on the other hand, was always "spot on" with timing and I could easily pick out dates in the past for changes of location or the ending of a relationship.

As the word spread, the psychics would line up at my table during breaks to get exact timing for the events that they intuitively knew were about to happen.

Those evenings were my classroom. I asked questions and found that clients would fill in the gaps. Book knowledge is the foundation of astrology, but it still requires practice, patience and listening for answers. As my skills developed, I could pick up on family abuse, serious illness of a parent, and other life-changing events.

One time I asked about an early relationship: "But you were only fifteen," I said.

"Arranged marriage," she told me.

"And two years later?"

"Divorce."

In addition to psychic circles, I read for friends and family.

I remember sitting at the house of a neighbor and telling her that her son was easygoing, personable, ambitious and smart.

"Your daughter, however, can be a little tough."

"Oh no," said Patti, "just the opposite."

I went home and hit the books trying to figure out where I had blundered but years later, she told me that my reading was absolutely correct.

Mistakes like that had made me doubt my abilities but after hundreds of readings, I got better at seeing the whole picture — and then I found a new problem.

The challenge was not just to read the chart but also to learn how to present this knowledge in a way that clients could embrace.

How to tell people that a desperately needed change is several years away? That they should finish up what's in progress before starting something new? That the romantic relationship they long for is not going to happen any time soon — or worse, that even if the right person were standing in front of them, they would find a way to mess it up.

This got worse as my skill in reading charts got better.

Back in the day, I assumed that my assessment was wrong, but now that I was sure — the frustration grew worse.

Too often I saw people who, despite being intelligent and outwardly successful, were unhappy and lacked any understanding of their deeper purpose in life and I saw them doing the same thing over and over, expecting a different outcome.

So how could a stranger speaking "truth" make a difference?

I considered going back to college to learn counseling skills, but life got in the way. A sick husband required me to run his business and keep things normal at home.

The burden grew heavier when he got hooked on opioid painkillers, went through surgery, and ran up massive debts.

Like other addicts, his biggest concern was for the fix and at night, he would shake me awake demanding to know where I'd stashed the supply. After a few weeks, I put a mattress on the floor in the walk-in closet and slept there – somewhat protected – but always with half an ear open for the sound of his footsteps and the pounding on the door.

He fell and broke his collarbone as a result of mixing Demerol with morphine patches and died in the hospital of an infection, several months later.

Looking back, I see only a blur of myself running as fast as I could to keep from being sucked into a black hole of medical emergencies and money problems, but his death left two houses in foreclosure, mounting debts and an ex-family that spewed anger and loathing

The next few years were difficult. It's never easy to be a single parent, but when you throw in grief, poverty and no health insurance, it becomes close to impossible.

It took courage to get up in the morning, and years to dig out of the hole – but I hung onto knowing that there were three separate positions in my chart that said financial abundance would arrive later in life.

It also helped that a friend offered me a job running the sales division of his small company and just as I had for my husband, I optimized the schedule by making appointments based on astrology.

I asked the salespeople to trust me. "Give me three or four days a week, and I will create success like you've never seen before."

With their approval, I booked calls for their most powerful days and avoided the times when it was difficult to make headway. They loved that I told them that on the "off" days (when the moon was void), they should do some paperwork and then go home.

Within a few weeks they were getting results, so I started sending calendars to friends and asking them to keep track.

One executive in a Fortune 500 company told me that he would close his door during the void times and put up a sticky-note saying:

"Back at 3.18 pm" (or whenever the void would end).

His productivity shot up — as did his reputation for being on time.

For myself, I trusted that my chart was correct and worked at translating and re-writing an ancient manuscript that I found in a second-hand bookstore in London. That book told me that I could find success in real estate, so I got my license and with astrology, figured out the correct timing for listing, showing and working with buyers.

Based on that, I knew in advance which showings would produce results and which ones would go nowhere and I learned to do my open houses on days when the cosmic timing was just right — and avoid the bad days and voids.

This gave me an edge and my listings sold (and rented) quickly which was a good thing as that gave me the time to write about astrology and do the research for this book.

All the insider secrets have evolved into an astrology program that tells you when to push forward — and when to take time off, slow down, relax and recharge.

Get a free trial and test it for yourself at:

LifeWellLived.net

Calendars, power days, life story reports, predictions and consults.

You can also see my daily astrology updates at Jenni Stone Astrologer on Facebook, or write to me at:

JenniStoneTheOne@gmail.com

Made in the USA
San Bernardino, CA
06 March 2020